Early American Children's Clothing and Textiles

Early American Children's Clothing and Textiles: Clothing a Child 1600–1800 explores the life experiences of Indigenous, Anglo-European, African, and mixed-race children in colonial America, their connections to textile production, the process of textile production, the textiles created, and the clothing they wore.

The book examines the communities and social structure of early America, the progression of the colonial textile industry, and the politics surrounding textile production beginning in the 1600s, with particular focus on the tasks children were given in the development of the American textile industry. The book discusses the concept of childhood in society during this time, together with documented stories of individual children. The discussion of early American childhood and textile production is followed by extant clothing samples for both boys and girls, ranging from Upper-class children's wear to children's wear of those with more humble means. With over 180 illustrations, the book includes images of textile production tools, inventions, and practices, extant textile samples, period portraits of children, and handmade extant clothing items worn by children during this time period.

Early American Children's Clothing and Textiles: Clothing a Child 1600–1800 will be of interest to working costume designers and technicians looking for primary historical and visual information for Early American productions, costume design historians, early American historians, students of costume design, and historical re-enactment costume designers, technicians, and hobbyists.

Carey Blackerby Hanson is Professor of Costume Design at the University of Mississippi. Her costume experience has covered a wide range of theatre, musical theatre, opera, dance, and theatre for youth. Carey has worked professionally with The Santa Fe Opera, Utah Opera, Sundance Summer Theatre, Old Lyric Repertory Company, Unicorn Theatre, The Pink Garter Theatre, and Playmill Theatre-Jackson. She is a member of the United States Institute for Theatre Technology and the Costume Society of America. As a costume historian, her research focus is early American children and textile production. She has traveled abroad as well as throughout the Eastern and Southern United States to gather primary information for her continuing research. With the support of the University of Mississippi department of Theatre and Film and the College of Liberal Arts, Carey is in the process of developing a historical clothing collection for students interested in studying extant garments.

Early American Children's Clothing and Textiles

Clothing a Child 1600–1800

—— CAREY BLACKERBY HANSON ——

Routledge
Taylor & Francis Group
NEW YORK AND LONDON

Designed cover image: © Photograph by Bob Watts. From the collections of the Museum of Old Newbury.

First published 2024
by Routledge
605 Third Avenue, New York, NY 10158

and by Routledge
4 Park Square, Milton Park, Abingdon, Oxon, OX14 4RN

Routledge is an imprint of the Taylor & Francis Group, an informa business

ISBN: 978-1-032-13691-2 (hbk)
ISBN: 978-1-032-13690-5 (pbk)
ISBN: 978-1-003-23044-1 (ebk)

DOI: 10.4324/9781003230441

Typeset in Bembo
by Apex CoVantage, LLC

I dedicate this book to my paternal grandparents:

William and Mary Ring
David and Jane O'Killia
William Walker and Mary Polly Hale
Emily Louella Hale Simpkins

Their personal histories are the inspiration behind this publication.

Contents

Acknowledgments

The research for this book would not have been possible without the support of the present and past chairs of the University of Mississippi Department of Theatre and Film and the College of Liberal Arts Summer Research Grant program. With funding from the Summer Research Grant program, I was given the opportunity to study early American children's garments in many wonderful museums and historical societies. Several of the extant children's clothing items I viewed are included in this publication.

A special thank you to Jennifer Swope, David and Roberta Logie, Associate Curator of Textile and Fashion Arts, Museum of Fine Arts, Boston, Rebecca Beall, Collections Manager and Curator of Textiles, Old Sturbridge Village; Connor Gaudet, Curator of Collections, Pilgrim Hall Museum; Dr. Laura Johnson, Linda Eaton Associate Curator of Textiles, Winterthur, Garden & Library; Stephanie Hebert, Collections Manager, Historic New England; Claire Senatore, Collections Manager and Kris Gaskins, Duxbury Rural and Historical Society; Kristen Fehlhaber, Assistant Director, Museum of Old Newbury; Vivien Barnett, Curatorial Assistant, Maryland Center for History and Culture; Linda Baumgarten, Curator of Textiles and Costumes, Colonial Williamsburg; and Noreen Marshall, Senior Curator, Museum of Childhood at the Victoria and Albert Museum.

In addition to the support of the University of Mississippi, I am thankful for Routledge Press and the wonderful mentors, colleagues, friends, and family who inspired me to do this research and encouraged me along the way. A heartfelt thank you to Nancy Hills, Rhona Justice-Malloy, Shea Howard, Jackie Fulmer, Linda Pisano, Jill Hoffman Cox, Kelly James Penot, Donna Buckley, Mary Ball, Lisa Wilson, and Mark Zachary. I am deeply grateful to Rhona Justice-Malloy, Shannon Zachary, Sydney Hanson Denmark, Michael Benge, and Zach Hanson Denmark who read and re-read the manuscript to help me shape, trim, and edit the final copy.

Most importantly, I would like to thank my husband and children, Dave Hanson, Evie Hanson, Sydney Hanson Denmark, and Aiden Hanson. Their never-ending patience allowed me to spend over a decade researching in art museums, living history museums, clothing and textiles collections, libraries, national heritage sites, historic villages, colonial era homes, historical societies, and in my home office as I prepared to write this book.

Introduction

From the beginning of colonization, all children of early America were impacted by the social and political systems surrounding them. Their life experiences varied greatly depending upon whether a child was Indigenous to the land, part of a British settlement project, or born into the colonial system of slavery. Often, the tasks children were assigned in the 17th and 18th centuries directly connected them to textiles and textile production. Over the years, very little has been published detailing children's lives in colonial times, their involvement in textile production, or the garments they were clothed in. This book will examine the life experiences of all children who lived in the colonies, their connections to textile production, the process of textile production leading up to the American Industrial Revolution, the textiles created, and the clothing they wore.

In the first quarter of the 1600s, through the lens of historical documentation and written personal accounts of English and European explorers, a collection of preserved stories describes the development of early British family settlements in North America. Captain John Smith wrote several books detailing his personal experiences in early Virginia. His volumes detail the adventures, as well as the extreme challenges, of the first men and boys sent to establish Jamestown in 1607.[1] Through the writings of Captain Robert Davies and Captain James Davies, readers are able to piece together the events which led to the failure of Popham colony, a sibling settlement to Jamestown that was established off the coast of Maine just a year after Jamestown's inception.[2] In addition to the stories of Jamestown and Popham colonies, time has kept the journal of William Bradford, Governor of Plymouth Plantation, intact. Bradford's consistent entries from 1608 through to 1646 paint a vivid picture of ordinary people, mostly comprised of family units, making their way from England to Holland and then to the Atlantic coast in 1620.[3]

Historically, these are invaluable written depictions of early American life. What is challenging about these documents is the fact that they were created by a collection of men who were accustomed to the cultural and social norms of England and Europe in the late 16th and early 17th centuries. What of the men, women, and children who had already made North America their home, well before the first European explorers stumbled upon the continent? While English and European explorers and settlers used pen and paper to record their experiences in this new world, Indigenous people of North America used spoken language to pass their cultural history down from one generation to the next. Over time, the Indigenous way of preserving history was overshadowed by written documentation. With the aid of archaeological

DOI: 10.4324/9781003230441-1

Figure 0.1 (Currier & Ives, *The Landing of the Pilgrims at Plymouth, Mass, Dec. 22nd, 1620*, ca 1876, lithograph, 33.3 x 44.5 cm (13.1 x 17.5 in), *Currier & Ives*, 1876. Library of Congress.)

evidence found in the 20th and 21st centuries, Indigenous history that had once been lost has slowly begun to resurface.

In New Mexico's White Sands National Park, footprints of Indigenous teenagers and younger children dating from approximately 21,000 to 23,000 years ago were recently uncovered. With this discovery, we now have evidence that Indigenous families were in existence in North America at the height of the last glacial occurrence, often referred to as the Last Glacial Maximum.[4] Additional archaeological findings detail that thousands of years before explorers from England and Europe found their way to the North American continent, 250 individually distinct Indigenous cultures spread throughout the Southeast, Northeast, Plains, Southwest, Great Basin, Northwest, and California regions of North America. Within the Northeast and Southeast landscape of late 16th century North America, there were an estimated 90 Indigenous cultures and six distinct languages.[5] Located on Block Island, just off the coast of Rhode Island, discovery of the Manissean village took place in the late 20th century. Excavation of the Indigenous site uncovered archaeological objects dating back to 1,000 BCE. These relics gave archaeologists a glimpse into the Iron Age of North America, dated before the development of Ancient Greece in the Mediterranean. The Manissean village, comprised of permanent family homes spanning a three-acre area, was a fishing and agricultural community established by the Niantic Indigenous people.[6]

On a much larger scale, the Cahokia Mounds, located just east of modern St. Louis, is the largest

Figure 0.2 Fossilized children's footprints discovered in White Sands National Park. (Dan Odess, 2019, photograph, White Sands, New Mexico. Courtesy of the National Park Service.)

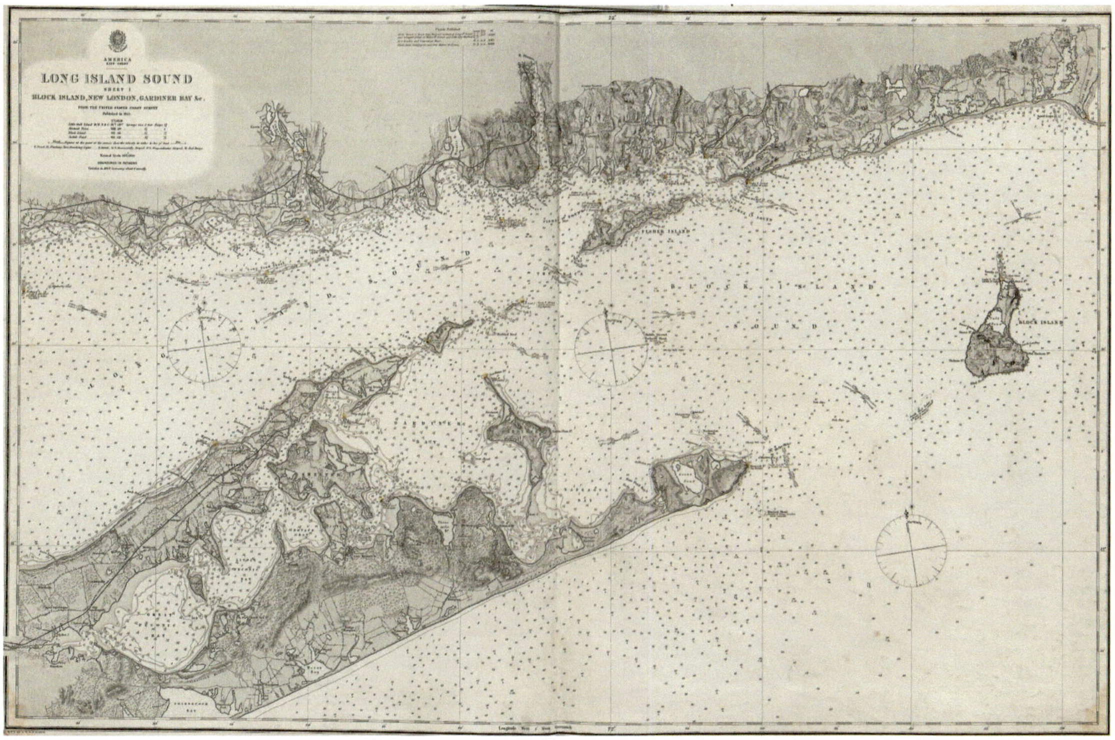

Figure 0.3 Nautical chart detailing the Long Island Sound and the location of Block Island. (Captain Williams, hydrographer, *Admiralty Chart No 2754 Long Island Sound Sheet 1 Block Island* (New London: Gardiner Bay & C, 1860) Wikimedia Commons.)

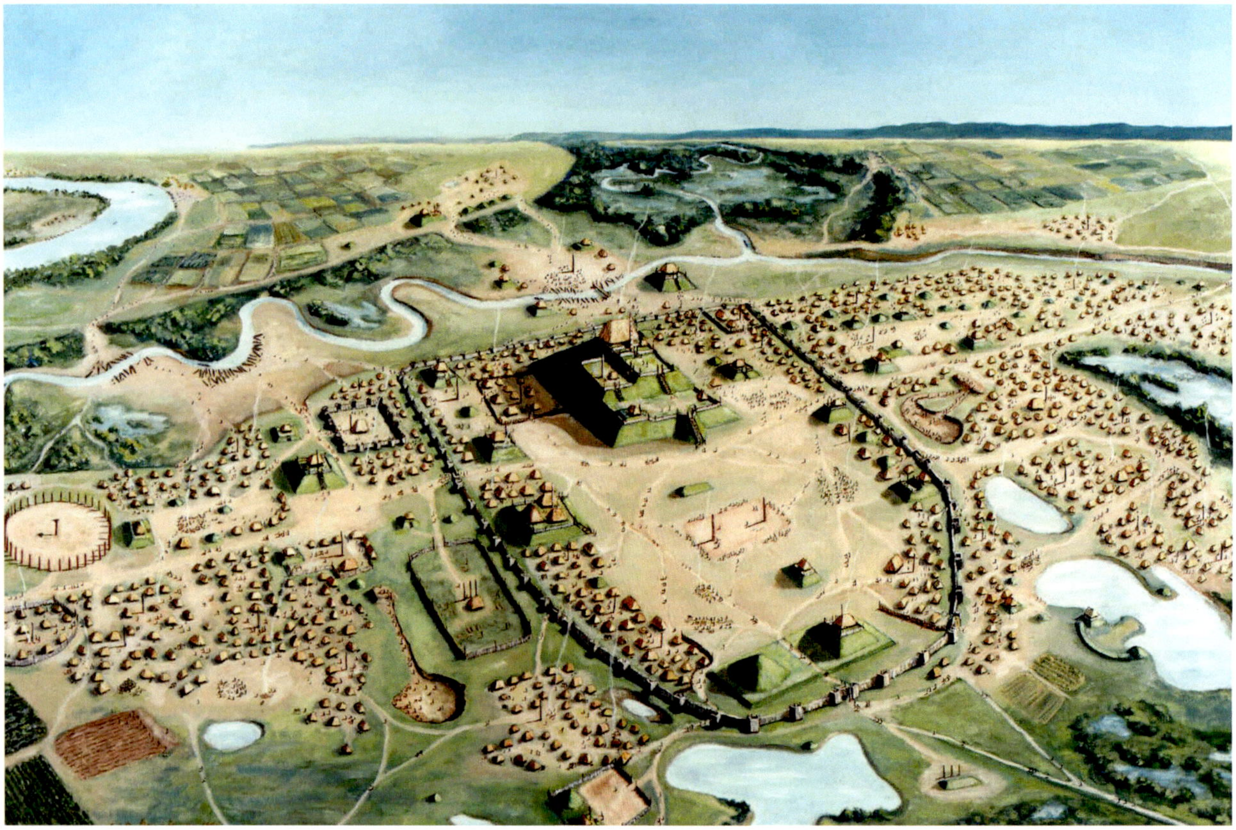

Figure 0.4 (William Iseminger, *Cahokia Mounds*, 1982, illustration, Collinsville, Illinois. Courtesy of the Cahokia Mounds State Historic Site.)

ancient Indigenous city of its kind yet to be discovered. Archaeological studies point to villages existing in and around this area by 600 AD.[7] Cahokia was not unlike our own modern cities, surrounded by individual suburbs, which then spread out into farming communities. At its peak, the Cahokia Mound was comprised of between 25,000 and 50,000 men, women, and children. Archaeologists have uncovered evidence of 120 mounds, plazas, public buildings, temples, and residential areas encompassing over six square miles.[8] Ancient Cahokia was both a thriving agricultural community and an influential center for trade in the Midwest region of North America.[9]

Through careful study of Cahokia and the surrounding early Indigenous villages, information concerning textile production was also discovered. According to these findings, fiber production was particularly plentiful between 1050 and 1100, when the population of the Cahokia region was at its largest. A unique building found under the Kunneman Mound in Cahokia held woven material, cordage, and fabric remnants made from finely spun threads. Ten miles east of Cahokia, at the site of Halliday village, a large quantity of ceramic disks with holes cut out of their centers were located. These disks, known as spindle whorls, were created from broken pottery and used to spin a variety of fibers in ancient Indigenous communities. The diameter of a spindle whorl corresponded to the fiber that was spun by the spinner. Smaller disks were used to spin fine animal hair and plant matter, while larger disks spun fibers from the slippery elm tree. Textiles in these Indigenous communities were produced for daily use as well as sacred rituals.[10]

Figure 0.5 Spindle whorl exhibit containing spindle whorl artifacts discovered at Cahokia Mounds State Historic Site. (Linda Sinco, photograph, Collinsville, Illinois. Courtesy of the Cahokia Mounds State Historic Site.)

Figure 0.6 North American spindle whorl dated between the 10th and 16th centuries. (Louis Petich Collection, ceramic, diameter 1–7/8 in (4.76 cm) New York. Courtesy of The Metropolitan Museum of Art.)

Comparing the Manissean village to Cahokia and its surrounding settlements, the size of early established Indigenous communities ranged from smaller villages to larger industrious cities. Sixteenth and 17th-century documentation has revealed there were an estimated 90,000 Indigenous men, women, and children living in settlements along the Atlantic coast before the first epidemic struck the region in 1619.[11] The colonists of the ill-fated Roanoke Colony recorded many interactions with the large Algonquian population, who lived and thrived in the Chesapeake Bay area. Artist John White and his scholarly colleague Thomas Harriot spent many months building relationships among the Algonquian people. Although the Roanoke settlement did not last, John White's drawings and Thomas Harriot's writings depicting well-established Algonquian villages did endure the passage of time as a detailed account of early Indigenous communities.[12]

British colonization in early 17th-century North America brought together two very different societies, both requiring land and resources for the success of their communities. One society was native to the land and the other wished to expand an existing empire on newly discovered soil. They each had different approaches to building and maintaining thriving communities, agricultural practices, family structures, political structures, social structures, customs, and traditions. To the leaders of British colonization, land was an asset to be controlled, bought, and sold.[13] In contrast, Indigenous

Figure 0.7 The Indigenous village Pomeiooc, located near present-day Lake Landing, North Carolina. Based on a watercolor created by John White. (Theodor de Bry, *The Towne of Pomeiooc*, 1590, engraving, 32.5 x 25.3 cm (12.7 x 9.9 in), *J. Wechel*, 1590. Courtesy of the John Carter Brown Library.)

Figure 0.8 Indigenous man and woman eating. Based on a watercolor by John White. (Theodor de Bry, *Their sitting at meate*, 1590, engraving, 15.2 x 21.2 (5.9 x 8.3 in), *J. Wechel*, 1590. Courtesy of the John Carter Brown Library.)

communities saw themselves tied to and responsible for the land they inhabited. Land was a living part of the sacred cycle of life, which included everything found on the land. All plants, animals, elements of the land, and humans were interconnected.[14] Both Queen Elizabeth I and King James I deeded this land, already settled by well-established Indigenous communities, to those chosen to represent England in North America. The monarchy gave little thought to the Indigenous men, women, and children who had cultivated and lived on the land for thousands of years.[15]

When the colonization of North America began, so did the introduction of Anglo-European children to the newly planned British settlements. The first nine English children, known to have arrived on the Atlantic coast in 1587, were part of the Roanoke Colony company. According to records, all nine children were boys. Two families each had one son, four men brought their own sons, and three additional boys seemed to have no family connections to anyone in the company. Shortly after their arrival in Virginia, two babies were born.[16] In the instance of both Jamestown and Popham colony in 1607, boys were sent under the supervision of adult men to begin establishing the early settlements. The first four boys sent to Jamestown traveled as servants to gentlemen who arrived on the first shipment. Jamestown would receive more children with the shipment of additional supplies and 500 colonists in 1609.[17] According to 17th-century written documentation, the most children to immigrate to early America arrived on the *Mayflower*. Among the 102 passengers to arrive on November 11, 1620, there were 35 children. Nineteen of the children were 12 or younger, with

Figure 0.09 Three Indigenous leaders of Florida. Based on a drawing by Jacques la Moyne de Morgues. (Theodor de Bry, *Was der Konig Vtina wann er in Krieg zeucht fur Kreigsordnung halt*, 1591, engraving, 15.2 x 20.9 cm (5.9 x 8.22 in) *Johann Feyerabendt*, 1591. Courtesy of the John Carter Brown Library.)

two babies who were born on the journey. Of the 35 children who began the journey, 17 of them would grow to adulthood and have families of their own in colonial America.[18] These extended families required more fabrics to clothe their growing children, which led to an ever-expanding need to produce textiles in colonial communities.

As fabric and clothing needs for colonial children increased, so did the need for labor in the textile creation process. The involvement of young children in the textile production process began with colonization and steadily grew as the late 18th century brought the Industrial Revolution to the early American textile industry.[19] The chapters in this book will discuss the political and social systems that impacted children, child labor, the development of the colonial textile production process, the role of children in that process, and children's clothing from the early 17th century through to the turn of the 19th century. Within each chapter, the information presented is broken down into three sections. The first sections of each chapter trace the effects of political and social structures on children, along with the increasing demand for child labor in colonial America. The second section of each chapter describes colonial textile production, the tools used in the production process, the textiles created, and the tasks given to children and adults based on gender. The final sections of each chapter detail clothing worn by all children living and working in early America.

Following this structure, the first section of chapter one explores the aggressive nature of British colonization and the use of Anglo-European, Indigenous, and African child labor to support settlement family units and communities.[20] The

Figure 0.10 Indigenous people of Florida planting crops for their community. Based on a drawing by Jacques la Moyne de Morgues. (Theodor de Bry, *Wei sie ire acker bauwen und beseen*, 1591, engraving, 14.7 x 21.2 cm (5.7 x 8.3 in) *Johann Feyerabendt*, 1591. Courtesy of the John Carter Brown Library.)

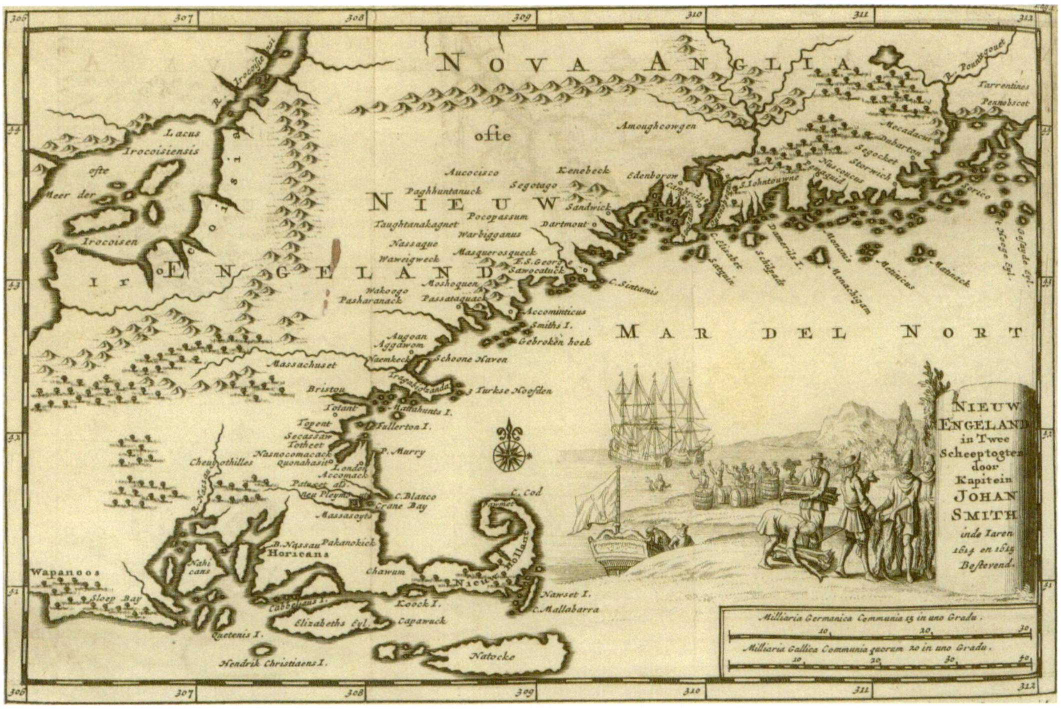

Figure 0.11 Map detailing the expanding colonization of New England. (*Nieuw Engeland in Twee Scheeptogten door Kapitein Johan Smith inde Iaren 1614 en 1615 Bestevend*, 1706, 15.4 x 23.5 cm (Leiden, Holland: Door Peter Vander, 1707.) Courtesy of the John Carter Brown Library.)

second section of chapter one details the methods and tools used in early 17th-century textile production, as well as the textiles that were created in the first colonial settlements. Children involved in textile and clothing production, regardless of their varying cultural backgrounds, learned the techniques Anglo-European settlers used in the creation of textiles and clothing.[21] Clothing practices of Indigenous children along the Atlantic coast, Anglo-European colonial children, and Indigenous children bound to service in Anglo-European homes are described in the last section of chapter one.

As the colonies expanded in the later 17th century, colonial systems of government began to harness child labor on a large scale in both northern and southern colonies. The beginning of chapter two describes the increasing use of Anglo-European poor, indentured, and orphaned children, along with Indigenous, African, and mixed-race children for physical labor.[22] With a newly dedicated focus on producing textiles, children of all economic and cultural backgrounds became an integral part of textile and clothing production.[23] The next section of chapter two details the growth of colonial textile production, the textiles created, the equipment used in the process, and the tasks children were given based on gender. Lastly, chapter two compares the clothing of all classes of Anglo-European colonial children with garments worn by Indigenous and African children bound to or enslaved by colonial households.

Soon after the establishment of all 13 colonies, laws began to categorize anyone of mixed Indigenous, African, or European ancestry as a slave to ensure a plantation economy based on free human labor.[24] Textiles were not only needed to clothe the colonial population but to purchase more African slaves to feed into the growing plantation system.[25] Chapter three examines the expanding colonial slave population of the early 18th century and the use of enslaved and poor children for physical labor and textile production. The textile section of chapter three details the use of textiles in the slave trade, the expansion of textile production, the textiles created, and ways in which colonial textiles could be dyed and hand printed. The textile section of chapter three also compares the fabrics used for the wealthy versus fabrics used to clothe the enslaved. Clothing practices varied for children depending upon their social class, cultural background, or if they were categorized as servants or slaves. The final section of chapter three compares the clothing of Indigenous people of the Atlantic coast and African slaves to the clothing of Anglo-European children in the colonies.

The final chapter of this book explores events leading up to, during, and after the American Revolution in relation to child labor and textile production. The first section describes political and social systems, the education of children, and child labor in all economic classes of the late 18th century. The textile section of the chapter chronicles the rapid increase in colonial textile production due to events leading up to the Revolutionary War, the development of the Industrial Revolution, and the establishment of the first textile mill in the United States. The second section of chapter four also details the newly formed textile industry's reliance on cotton plantation children of the South and textile mill children of the North.[26] Chapter four ends the book with descriptions of clothing items worn by Anglo-European children of all social classes in contrast to the clothing of Indigenous servant and African enslaved children at the turn of the 19th century.

NOTES

1 John Smith, *A Map of Virginia: With a Description of the Countrey, the Commodities, People, Government, and Religion*, ed. Thomas Abbay (Oxford: Joseph Barnes, 1612), Internet Archive; John Smith, *The Generall Historie of Virginia, New England & the Summer Isles: Together with the True Travels, Adventures and Observations, and A Sea Grammar* (Glasgow: J. MacLehose, 1907), Library of Congress.

2 Henry O. Thayer, *The Sagadahoc Colony: Comprising the Relation of a Voyage into New England* (Portland: Gorges

Society, 1892), Google Books; Captain James Davies, *A Relation of Voyage to Sagadahoc, Edited with Preface Notes and Appendix*, ed. B. F. Decosta (Cambridge: Johnson Wilson and Son, University Press, 1880), Google Books.

3 William Bradford, *The History of Plymouth Plantation*, ed. Charles Deane (Cambridge: Brown Little, 1856), Google Books.

4 Maya Wei-Haas, "Stunning Footprints Push Back Human Arrivals in Americas by Thousands of Years," *National Geographic*, September 23, 2021, Internet Article.

5 Josephine Paterek, *Encyclopedia of American Indian Costume* (New York: W. W. Norton & Company, 1993), 5, 41, 49, 83, 147, 189, 209, 243, 293, 345, 383.

6 Kathleen J. Bragdon, *Native People of Southern New England, 1500–1650* (Norman: University of Oklahoma Press, 1996), 34, 66.

7 Timothy R. Pauketat, "Refiguring the Archaeology of Greater Cahokia," *Journal of Archaeological Research* 6, no. 1 (March 1998): 45–47, 49, 74, www.jstor.org/stable/41053152.

8 William R. Iseminger, "St. Louis: The Cahokia Mounds Phenomenon: America's Ancient City," *History News* 59, no. 1 (Winter 2004): 26–27, www.jstor.org/stable/42655506.

9 Pauketat, "Refiguring the Archaelogy," 48.

10 Susan Alt, "Spindle Whorls and Fiber Production at Early Cahokian Settlements," *Southeastern Archaeology* 18, no. 2 (Winter 1999): 124–30, www.jstor.org/stable/40713163.

11 Bragdon, *Native People: 1500–1650*, 26.

12 Richard Middleton and Anne Lombard, *Colonial America: A History to 1763*, 4th ed. (West Sussex: Wiley-Blackwell, 2011), 43; Thomas Harriot, *A Brief and True Report of the New Found Land of Virginia*, ed. Paul Royster (London: University of Nebraska-Lincoln, 1588), 34–46, Digital Commons@University of Nebraska-Lincoln.

13 Bragdon, 16.

14 Rebecca Tsosie, "Land, Culture, and Community: Reflections on Native Sovereignty and Property in America," *Indiana Law Review* 34 (Winter 2001): 1291–93.

15 Rev. Carlos Shatter, *Sir Humfrey Glylberte and His Enterprise of Colonization in America* (Boston: Prince Society, 1903), 95–102, The Avalon Project; William Waller Hening, *The Statutes at Large; Being a Collection of All the Laws of Virginia from the First Session of the Legislature, in the Year 1619*, vol. 1 (New York: R. & W. & G. Bartow, 1823), 57–66, The Avalon Project.

16 William S. Powell, "Roanoke Colonists and Explorers: An Attempt at Identification," *The North Carolina Historical Review* 34, no. 2 (April 1957): 202–26, www.jstor.org/stable/23516851.

17 Mary Newton Standard, *Colonial Virginia Its People and Customs* (Philadelphia: J. B. Lippincott Company, 1917), 32, Google Books.

18 John J. Navin, "Decrepit in Their Early Youth: English Children in Holland and Plymouth Plantation," in *Children in Colonial Times*, ed. James Marten (New York: New York University Press, 2007), 131.

19 Ruth Wallis Herndon and John E. Murray, eds., *Children Bound to Labor: The Pauper Apprentice System in Early America* (Ithaca: Cornell University Press, 2009), 202.

20 Ann Marie Plane, *Colonial Intimacies: Indian Marriage in Early New England* (Ithaca: Cornell University Press, 2000), 65.

21 Norman Earl Tanis, "Education in John Eliot's Indian Utopias, 1646–1675," *History of Education Quarterly* 10, no. 3 (1970): 317, https://doi.org/10.2307/367526.

22 Alan Gallay, *The Indian Slave Trade: The Rise of the English Empire in the American South, 1670–1717* (New Haven: Yale University Press, 2002), 57; Peter H. Wood, *Black Majority* (New York: W. W. Norton & Company, 1974), 39; Denise I. Bossy, "Godin & Co.: Charleston Merchants and the Indian Trade, 1674–1715," *The South Carolina Historical Magazine* 114, no. 2 (2013): 97.

23 Thomas J. Wertenbaker, *The Planters of Colonial Virginia* (Princeton: Princeton University Press, 1922), 108.

24 Daragh Grant, "'Civilizing' the Colonial Subject: The Co-Evolution of State and Slavery in South Carolina, 1670–1739," *Comparative Studies in Society and History* 57, no. 3 (2015): 619, www.jstor.org/stable/43908365.

25 Sven Beckert, *Empire of Cotton* (New York: Vintage Books, 2015), 36, 45–46.

26 Herndon and Murray, *Children Bound to Labor*, 202–3.

CHAPTER ONE

1600–1660

To understand the world children found themselves in the first half of the 17th century in early America, this chapter will explore the social and family structures of well-established Indigenous communities and newly formed colonial settlements. Within each cultural tradition, children were given specific duties, based on their gender at birth, to assist in the building and preserving of their communities. As British colonization progressed, child labor became increasingly essential and was often viewed as a commodity. In addition to children working to stabilize their own family units, poor and indentured children were sent from England and Europe to serve as labor in colonial settlements. Regional Indigenous children sold into slavery or taken to 'civilize' as part of a Puritan mission project were also used as labor in early settlements, as were African children with the onset of the transatlantic slave trade.[1] Producing a variety of homespun textiles and traditional clothing for a growing colonial population quickly became a labor-heavy endeavor in the home and in the community. The creation of textiles and clothing in early America mirrored the methods and techniques settlers were accustomed to in their countries of origin. Clothing for settler children often reflected British and European traditional styles and construction of the early 17th century. While the Indigenous populations of North America embraced their own unique practices of textile and clothing production, those used as labor in settlement homes or in Puritan mission projects were taught to produce textiles and dress in what was deemed the 'appropriate' Anglo-European way.[2]

COMMUNITIES: SOCIAL AND POLITICAL STRUCTURE

INDIGENOUS COMMUNITIES

Indigenous communities of the 17th-century Atlantic coast consisted of men, women, and children of all ages. Family units of mothers, fathers, children, grandparents, aunts, uncles, and cousins connected in a system of kinship within each village. The strongest bonds between Indigenous men and women were clan affiliation and kinship.[3] Kinship traditions connected the individual to the family, the family unit to the community, and each community to the Indigenous nation as a whole.[4] Early North American Atlantic coast kinship communities included the Massachusett, Pennacook, Nauset, Wampanoag, Narragansett, Wappinger, Pequot, Mohegan, Niantic, Pawtuxet, Powohatan, Delaware, Conoy, Montauk, Secotan, Roanoke, Pamlico, Croatan, and Tuscarora people.[5]

DOI: 10.4324/9781003230441-2

A majority of southern New England Indigenous families lived in moderate-sized villages. Women farmed the land with the aid of their children close to family homesteads, while men fished, hunted, trapped, and traded, away from the village. Children undertook tasks associated with their gender at birth. Female children learned from their mothers to raise crops, gather wild plants, store food, cook, construct homes, tan animal hides, make clothing, and create pottery. They were also taught the art of weaving mats, bags, and baskets. Male children learned skills from their fathers. They were trained to use a bow and arrow, expertly fish, hunt, trap birds, trade with other Native communities, create tools, as well as carve canoes, and household utensils.[6] Grandparents, parents, siblings, and close relatives all carried responsibilities for teaching Indigenous children social and cultural traditions. It was of the utmost importance that a child grew up in a nurturing environment to gain a positive view of what it meant to be part of a family, a village, a band, and an Indigenous nation.[7]

The social hierarchy system in which early Indigenous children were raised seems to have functioned on a multi-tier structure. The leader of the community, known as a sachem, along with his or her family, held the highest status. Next in the social hierarchy came the advisers and counselors to the sachem or chief. Under the advisers and counselors were the common people of the community, servants, and individuals who were not considered part of the social class system.[8] Archaeological evidence of this social order coincides with what has been discovered at Cahokia Mounds both in housing structures and burial mounds.[9] In a large percentage of permanent Indigenous villages a matrilineal system was used to determine leadership in a community. In a matrilineal structure, Indigenous leadership roles

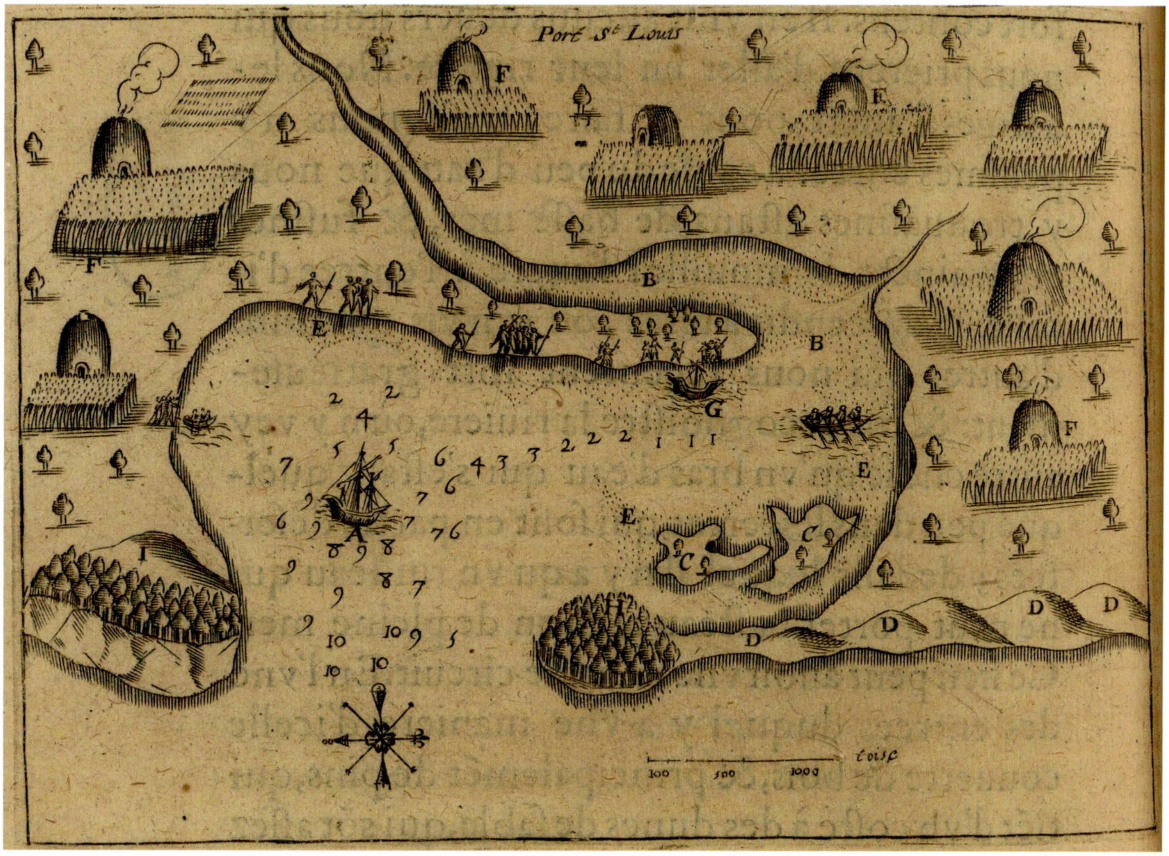

Figure 1.1 Map detailing 17th-century Indigenous villages of Plymouth Bay, Massachusetts. (Samuel de Champlain, cartographer, *Port St. Louis*, 1613, 10.7 x 14.8 cm, (Paris: Chez Iean Berjon, 1613). Courtesy of the John Carter Brown Library.)

Figure 1.2 The Indigenous town of Secotan. Based on a watercolor by John White. (Theodor de Bry, *The Town of Secota*, 1590, engraving, 31.1 x 23.1 cm (12.2 x 9 in). Courtesy of the John Carter Brown Library.)

came down through a woman's lineage, while other clans allowed women held in high honor to play a crucial role in choosing the next leader.[10] Historical records indicate that a majority of the Indigenous sachems were male, however, and evidence does exist of female sachems in the 17th cetury.[11]

BRITISH COLONIALIZATION

British leaders began to quickly realize peace with Indigenous sachems was critical in exchange for land they wished to claim as their own.[12] In March of 1620, Governor William Bradford made a diplomatic effort to make peace with Massasoit, the paramount sachem of the Wampanoags, to secure the land for Plymouth colony. His efforts were awarded with a 24-year alliance with the Wampanoag people.[13] These first verbal land negotiations were witnessed by leaders of the British settlements and Indigenous clans. As time passed, colonial settlers began documenting accounts of verbal agreements as proof of land negotiations with Indigenous leaders, regardless of whether the conversations actually

Figure 1.3 Illustration of Chief Massasoit and his warriors with Governor William Bradford. (*Massasoit and His Warriors*, 1857, wood engraving, Library of Congress.)

took place. These written accounts became known as 'Indian deeds' by British colonists.[14]

As British colonization continued in the early 17th century, political unrest, economic depression, disease, and poverty made life in Britain and Europe unbearable for many. Due to these circumstances, in 1629, a large number of families with children began pouring across the Atlantic as part of the Massachusetts Bay Colony project.[15] With this uptick in mostly middle-class Puritan families from east England, more land was required to house them. As time progressed, negotiating land ownership with Indigenous sachems to establish new colonial townships ended. England began granting North American land to colonists first, then came the process of negotiating for an 'Indian deed,' which was recorded by the General Court system. Regardless of whether the sachem in a particular area verbally agreed to allow English settlers to claim land or not, the Massachusetts court system now used legal means to secure property without Indigenous approval.[16] By 1640, approximately 80,000 men, women, and children had traveled across the Atlantic to the British colonies in North America. Colonial settlements began to surround Indigenous villages.[17]

When examining which early British settlements succeeded in the beginning stages of colonization and which did not, it becomes clear that, without assistance from neighboring Indigenous communities, the early colonies would not have survived. Unfortunately, due to the traditional social customs of England, many appointed settlement leaders from the elite class did not see the Indigenous people as equals of their modern sophisticated society.[18]

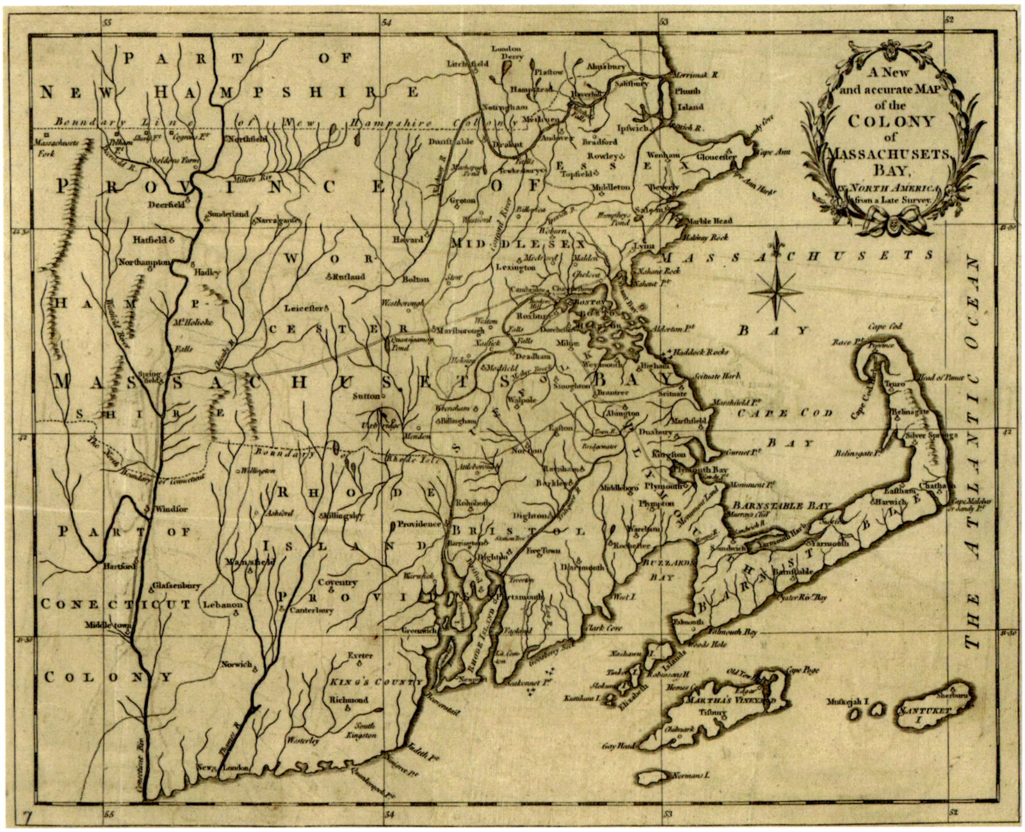

Figure 1.4 Map of Massachusetts Bay Colony in 1780. (John Hinton, cartographer, *A new and accurate map of the colony of Massachusetts Bay, in North America, from a late survey*, 1780, 25 x 32 cm (London: John Hinton, 1780) Library of Congress.)

The hierarchy of who was and was not deemed equal stemmed from 16th-century social traditions based on wealth and privilege. The monarch was placed on the highest tier, followed by a small elite group of nobility and a lesser class of gentry. Next in social status was the yeoman class, comprised of landowners, tenant farmers, shopkeepers, and artisans, followed by the class of manual laborers. The lower class was comprised of apprentices and servants, ending with the impoverished and the destitute.[19]

ANGLO-EUROPEAN INDENTURED SERVANTS

Establishing early settlements was labor intensive as well as fraught with disease, starvation, and conflicts with neighboring Indigenous communities. Under these extreme conditions, many of the first shipments of colonists did not survive. Among those who perished, as well as labored intensely for survival, were indentured servants bound and contracted to serve the colonies.[20] The indentured servants of early America were individual men, women, and children willingly or unwillingly bound by a labor contract to another person, group, or colony for a specific term of service. The longest length of service was usually seven years for the English or European settler population.[21] Those forcibly shipped to the colonies as indentured servants experienced a variety of difficult circumstances. Profit-minded English merchants often arranged for the abduction of young men, women, and children from the streets of London and Dublin for sale into indentured servitude.[22]

Figure 1.5 Illustration of Englishmen negotiating with Chief Powhatan in his village. (Theodor de Bry, *Ralph Hamor asks for the hand of Powhatan's daughter*, 1706, engraving, 13.7 x 18.4 cm (5.3 x 7.2 in). Courtesy of the John Carter Brown Library.)

The early colonies also followed the English practice of binding out poor children from their homes into service elsewhere. Between 1618 and 1622, numerous impoverished English children were transported to Virginia from London. Documentation from 1620 describes the arrangement of 100 poor London children shipped to Virginia as indentured servants, against their will.[23] Parish officers and magistrates determined which children could stay in their lower-income English homes and which children should be bound out for service. Due to the labor needed in colonial settlements, poor parents were often coerced into giving up their children. Parish officials often threatened to stop poor relief to impoverished parents unless they agreed to send several of their children to the colonies.[24] Over time, children became the largest number of those in colonial servitude.[25]

INDIGENOUS LABOR

Before 1637, European indentured servant labor began to decrease, which steadily dropped until 1680 when it plummeted altogether.[26] With the rising need for labor in the colonies, and a falling European indentured servant pool, settlement leaders looked for replacement labor in closer proximity. Leading up to 1637, tensions between the Pequot people, the Narragansett people, and the Massachusetts Bay Colony settlers escalated as land became crowded with colonial settlements and food was scarce.[27] On a morning in April, 1637, the Narragansett people and the Connecticut militia, with the approval of the Massachusetts Bay Colony leaders, attacked a large Pequot village. Most of the Indigenous adult men were gone the morning of

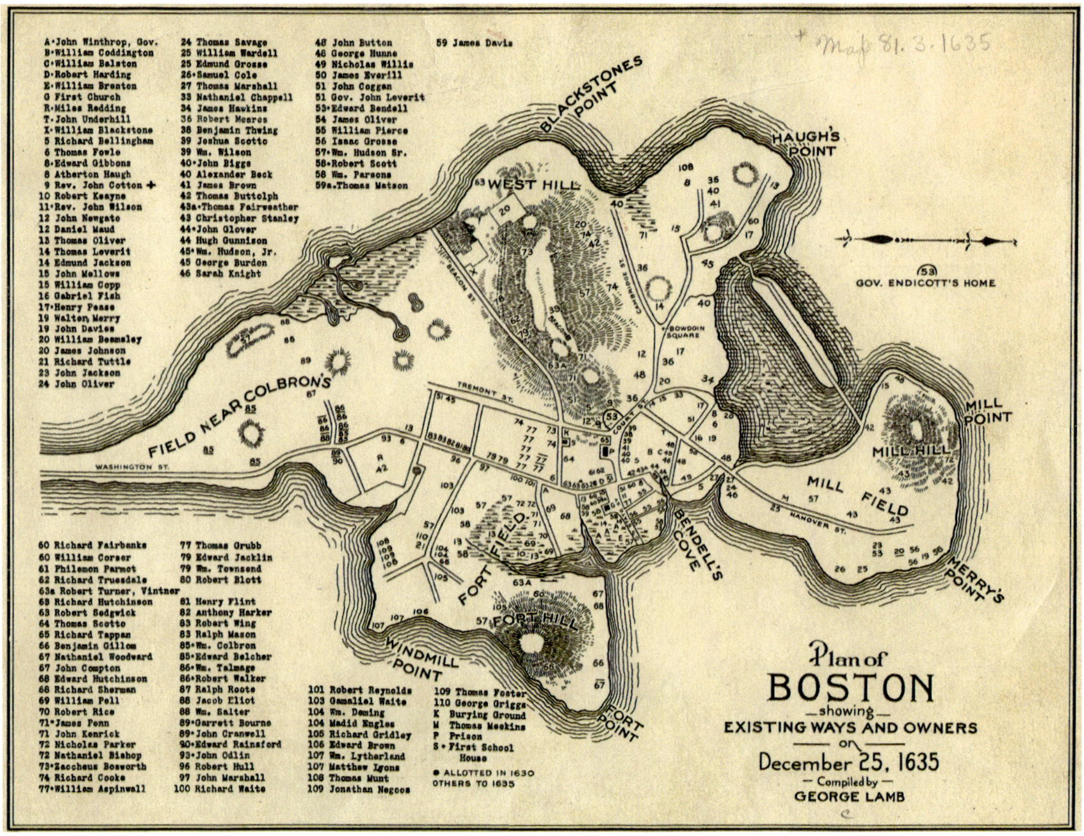

Figure 1.6 Map detailing the location of Boston households Pequot captives were sold to.

(George Lamb, cartographer, *Plan of Boston showing existing ways and owners on December 25, 1635*, 1928, 20 x 25 cm (Boston: William Nichols Mears, 1928), Boston Public Library).

the attack. Under the command of English Captain John Mason, most of the women, children, and older people of the village were killed. Similar raids against the Pequots continued for months until a majority of the Pequot men had been executed. The surviving women and children, numbering close to 300, found themselves sold at a public auction and forced into service in the homes of Massachusetts Bay Colony Puritan families.[28] In many instances, the adult women captives were bound for ten years, while the children were bound until the age of 25. Some captives, however, were bound for life, per orders of the General Court system, or later willed to relatives for a continued life of service.[29]

INDIGENOUS PRAYING TOWNS

In addition to Indigenous slavery practices, planned efforts organized by Puritan ministers and the English government began to break apart Indigenous cultural and family kinship traditions at the onset of colonialism. With the development of the New England Company in 1649 and the support of the Massachusetts General Court, land and funding were gifted to Puritan Reverend John Eliot for the creation of Indigenous 'praying towns.'[30] In these towns, male Indigenous villagers were taught to read and write English, to understand Massachusetts laws and Christian theology, as well as learn craft skills and farming. Indigenous females were instructed in the traditional domestic skills expected of an English woman.[31] The philosophy behind 'praying towns' was to convert Indigenous people both spiritually and culturally.[32] All 14 towns established in Massachusetts Bay Colony were separated from English communities as well as the Indigenous communities the villagers had previously inhabited.[33] Natick, the first well-documented 'praying town,' was located 18 miles southwest of Boston.[34] Indigenous men, women, and children who found themselves isolated in these organized villages eventually became disowned by their own people as well as disregarded by an English society who would not accept them. They could never go back to their family and kin, nor could they move forward in colonial society.[35]

AFRICAN LABOR

Although the first African laborers were sold in Virginia in 1619, the African slave labor system was not fully in place until the establishment of the Royal African Company in 1672. Until that point, colonists with the economic means relied on a mixed group of European indentured servants, African labor, and Indigenous bound servants to work in the fields and in their homes.[36] Colonists quickly discovered that Indigenous people, enslaved

Figure 1.7 (Felix Octavius Carr Darley, *John Eliot Preaching to the Indians*, illustration, 15 3/16 x 19 1/4 in. (38.6 x 48.9 cm), (Philadelphia: Gleasons Pictorial, 1822–1888), gift of Martha J. Fleischman and Barbara G. Fleischman, 1999. Courtesy of The Metropolitan Museum of Art.)

Figure 1.8 Illustrated view of Natick, the first 'praying town.' (George E. Norris, *Cochituate, Massachusetts and North Natick*, 1887, illustration, 49 x 66 cm (19.2 x 25.9 in), Library of Congress.)

in a region they were familiar with, could easily escape to neighboring Indigenous tribes for protection. Indigenous slaves were also not immune to European diseases, which killed many Indigenous captives needed for labor.[37] According to Governor Winthrop's records, in July 1637, Captain William Pierce took 15 captive Indigenous Pequot boys and two Indigenous women for trade to Providence Island on a ship called *Desire*. When Pierce returned to Massachusetts in February 1638, his cargo included cotton, tobacco, and African labor. This new system of trading captive Indigenous men, women, and children for African labor on the international slave market paved the way for the development of a large-scale African slave trade in the colonies.[38] Indigenous captives who were not bound to servitude were now used as commodity for networking on the expanding transatlantic slave trade system.[39]

Massachusetts Bay became the first colony in New England to fully participate in the African slave trade, while also continuing to sell Indigenous captives.[40] Indigenous servitude and slavery, as well as trading Indigenous people for African slaves, grew in New England. Tens of thousands of probate records, in Suffolk County alone, document a mix of African and Indigenous men, women, and children in bondage.[41] The life circumstances of these individuals were listed in the inventories of their masters, written down in personal journals, or recorded in bills of sale.[42] Through these 17th-century documents, proof of involvement in both Indigenous and African child labor can clearly be seen. Probate inventories often list the names of the children, whether they were 'Negro,' 'Indian,' or 'Molatto,' as well as how many years they were to serve after the death of their owner. In many instances, estate records document a mix of ethnically diverse children bound to one master.[43]

NEW ENGLAND HOUSEHOLDS

In the Massachusetts Bay Colony, a large percentage of the male population were small farmers or skilled in a manual trade.[44] Most Puritan families housed four to six children in a household at any given time, with an emphasis placed on the core structure of father, mother, and children.[45] In the patriarchal English colonial home, men were heads of the household with their wives and children subject to their authority. Marriages were not based on affection but rather on social rank and suitability. When colonial marriages were approved by parents or guardians and children were born, young parents were expected to provide food, shelter, and protection for their children.[46] Based on the theology of John Calvin, Puritans believed all infants were born unenlightened and naturally drawn to inappropriate behavior. The focus of raising children in a Puritan home was to 'break the will' of the child. This was carried out through strict supervision, usually under the leadership of the father.[47]

Both male and female children in the English Puritan home were given gender-specific tasks by the age of six or seven. Boys began working with the father of the household, while girls began learning domestic skills from the mother.[48] Between the ages of ten and 14, boys were expected

Figure 1.9 Photograph of the Jonathan Fairbanks House of Dedham, Massachusetts, built in 1636. Jonathan and his wife Grace raised six children in the Fairbanks House. (Stanley Mixon and Thomas T. Waterhouse, 1933, *Jonathan Fairbanks House, 511 East Street, Dedham, Norfolk County, MA*, photograph, *Historic American Buildings Survey*, June 1936, Library of Congress.)

to choose a career path and begin an apprenticeship, which lasted seven years. Girls continued to train in the skills of housewifery and gardening in preparation for becoming wives and mothers.[49] To help with day-to-day labor, many early colonial households employed an indentured English or European servant bound to the family for five to seven years.[50] Due to the decline of indentured servitude, additional labor in Puritan homes began to shift to Indigenous servants and slaves. By the 1650s, Indigenous children living in 'praying towns' with their families were sent away to serve in Puritan homes, after completing their English education.[51] Ministers and authorities encouraged and sometimes forced Indigenous parents to place their children in bound service to English families. Placing Indigenous children in Puritan homes further separated them from their Native culture in order to 'civilize' them.[52]

TEXTILES AND TEXTILE PRODUCTION

Since the reign of Henry VIII, London was the dominant port for exporting English and European textiles to the world.[53] With the establishment of the colonies, British and European merchants saw a lucrative opportunity in shipping fabrics to the Atlantic coast. As with most colonists' families, textiles were an important part of the household. In the 1631 probate inventory of Plymouth colonist Mary Ring, yardages of kersey, colored moll, blue cloth, green cloth, say cloth, and linen were recorded. Items made from textiles within her possession included sheets, table napkins, tablecloths, pillow coverings, blankets, curtains, coverlets, and a variety of clothing items.[54] Knowing the importance of textiles, England quickly shipped a variety of fabrics to the colonies for purchase at the onset of settlement. In the Massachusetts Bay Colony, stores were established for colonists to buy goods including clothing, fabric by the yard, and blankets. In 1646, the shop of Captain Joseph Weld offered a variety of colored cottons, coarse woolen, kersey, broadcloth, flannel, fustian, penniston, Holland, slezie lawn, frize, and linen. Altogether, the fabric inventory of Captain Weld totaled over 600 yards of cloth.[55] The colonies were to supply England with raw materials, but not to create their own products from the raw materials they gathered or produced. Colonists were to be consumers of English manufactured goods not to manufacture items for themselves.

Contrary to this imposed economic structure, many English colonists immigrating to North America were arriving with the knowledge and experience of producing textiles. The practice of creating homespun cloth in English households had been passed down for many generations. Housewives often produced the textile needs of the family to help maintain a thrifty budget.[56] Many Plymouth colonists and their children, before arriving on the Atlantic coast, were previously employed in the Leiden textile industry.[57] After arriving in the colonies, separatist families were teaching girls by the age of six or seven to spin fibers into yarn in Plymouth homes.[58] During the Great Migration between 1630 and 1643, many men skilled in flax dressing, weaving, and fulling made their way to the colonies as well.[59] The first known established community of cloth makers was recorded in Rowley, Massachusetts. In 1638, several of the Rowley settlers, who arrived with Reverend Ezekiel Rogers, had been clothiers in England. Not only were the adults involved in cloth production; their young children were taught to spin cotton and wool.[60]

Soon after Rowley was established, the number of immigrants arriving in the colonies dropped due to improved living conditions in England. As immigration decreased, so did the number of shipments of goods coming from England, which included much-needed textiles.[61] Seeing the need for textile production within the colonies, the General Court

Figure 1.10 (Geertruydt Roghman, *A Woman Spinning, Plate 4 from Five Feminine Occupations*, 1640–1657, engraving, 8 3/16 x 6 1/2 in (20.8 x 16.5 cm), the Elisha Whittelsey Collection, the Elisha Whittelsey Fund, 1956. Courtesy of The Metropolitan Museum of Art).

of Massachusetts Bay ordered town magistrates in May 1640, to gather information concerning how to produce textiles in the area and who in their communities were skilled in spinning fibers and weaving. Further instructions focused on teaching young boys and girls to spin fibers into yarn. Nine months later, the General Court ordered each family within the colony to grow flax and hemp in order to produce linen cloth. At the same time, another order was given for plantations in the colony to begin cultivating cotton once a shipment of the plants arrived from the West Indies.[62]

THE BEGINNING OF COLONIAL TEXTILE PRODUCTION

This push toward textile production in the colonies coincided with the establishment of the first fulling mill in 1643. The fulling mill was constructed for finishing wool cloth produced by the community of cloth makers in Rowley.[63] Soon after the first fulling mill was up and running, in 1645, the General Court ordered more sheep to be brought from England and that all towns must increase the number of sheep within their communities.[64] As textile production expanded, so did the need for more colonists to take part in the work. By 1656, the General Court ordered all women, boys, and girls to spin wool, cotton, and flax for cloth production. In addition, the executive order outlined how many pounds of fibers should be spun each week per family.[65] Virginia was also involved in early textile production. Housewives of early Virginian homes were recorded as weaving linen for bedding and producing clothing out of a cloth known as 'Virginia Cloth.'[66] Similarly to Massachusetts, Virginia created a system of cloth making in the 1640s by

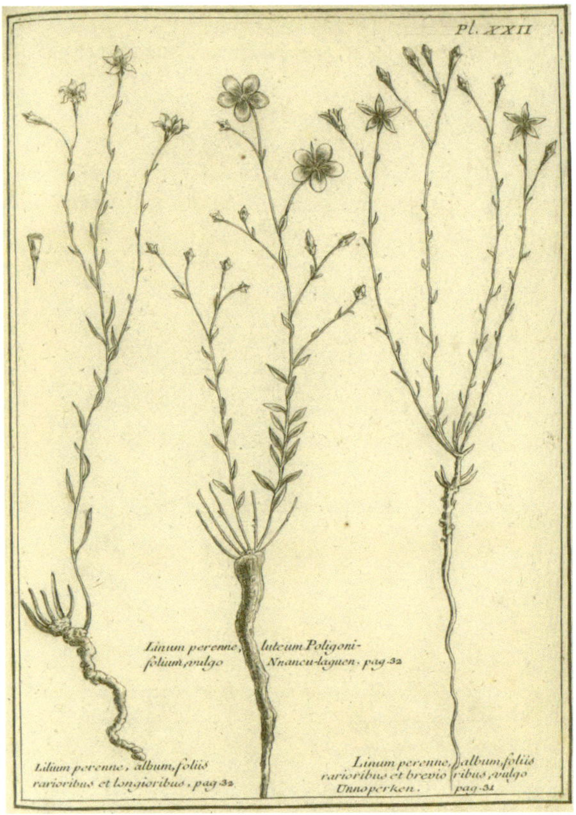

Figure 1.11 Illustration of early America flax plants. (Louis Feuillee, 1711, engraving, 21.3 x 15 cm (8.3 x 5.9 in), *Pierre Giffart*, 1725. Courtesy of the John Carter Brown Library.)

Figure 1.12 Site of Stony Brook, Massachusetts, fulling mill established in 1664. The fulling mill burned in 1760 and was replaced by a wool mill. (Historic American Buildings Survey, *Stony Brook Mill, Old Coach Road, Brewster, Barnstable County, MA*, 1933, photograph, Library of Congress.)

establishing public flax houses for manufacturing linen. With the growing need to create more textiles, in 1646, Virginia lawmakers saw the need to order poor children to serve as additional labor. The Grand Assembly passed a law authorizing appointed commissioners to bind out poor children from their families to work in these public flax houses.[67]

The primary fabrics produced in the colonies consisted of hemp, flax, cotton, and wool. *New England's First Fruits*, published in 1643, reported the success of growing flax and hemp for the purpose of spinning and weaving linen cloth.[68] Long silky fibers of the hemp and flax plant were used to make linen, while the shorter and rougher tow fibers of the flax plant produced a heavy canvas-like fabric.[69] Osnaburg was a durable and strong unbleached plain weave linen used for a variety of purposes in early America. It was often used in the colonies for sacks as well as servants' and slaves' clothing.[70] In 1640, cotton was introduced as a textile fiber to the colonies through trade relations with Barbados. Barbados was the first West Indies Island to produce cotton on a large scale for export. The specific type of cotton traded with the American colonies was first planted there in 1627. Cotton, or 'cotton woole,' as it was often called, became a large export for Barbados, equal to tobacco.[71] *New England's First Fruits* details the use of 'cotton woole' fibers, bought from the islands for a reasonable cost. The island cotton was prepared, cleaned, carded, spun, and woven together with linen to create fustian and dimity. The two fabrics created from this

Figure 1.13 Cotton hand carders used to prepare cotton fibers for the spinning process. (Old Whitmore Cotton No. A10 cotton hand carders, 19th century, wood, from the O.B. and Sue S. Annis Estate, gift of L. Ray Baker. Courtesy of the Panhandle-Plains Historical Museum.)

cotton and linen blend were used for summer clothing in early America.[72]

TEXTILE AND CLOTHING PRODUCTION IN THE COLONIAL HOME

Early production of flax and wool-based cloth in the family home involved the labor of women and their children. When producing wool cloth, the wool fibers were first carded using hand cards to comb through and align the fibers. Once carding was complete, the wool fibers were spun on a hand wheel, which turned the combed fibers into yarn. The yarn could then be woven into cloth using a handloom.[73] One of the most produced textiles in the home was a fabric that combined linen in the warp of the cloth and wool in the weft. This mixed cloth proved to be strong from the use of linen and soft due to the carded wool. 'Linsey-woolsey' was used for clothing, blankets, bedding, and curtains.[74] Linen woven by itself was often used in undergarments, shirts, sheets, tablecloths, dresses, and handkerchiefs. The process of making linen cloth was similar to making wool cloth. Once the fibers were combed, they were wrapped and loosely tied around a tool used for spinning, known as a distaff. From the distaff, the fibers were drafted and spun into yarn using a hand wheel or a foot-operated linen wheel. From there, the spun flax yarn was woven together on the loom.[75] As textile production increased, so did the number of spinning wheels in early New England homes. According to probate inventories, before 1649, only 15 percent

Figure 1.14 Illustration of a woman holding a distaff full of fibers. (Jean-Baptiste Greuxe, *Peasant Girl with a Distaff,* 1755, drawing, 7 15/16 x 5 3/8 in (20.2 x 13.6 cm), Harry G. Sperling Fund, 1982. Courtesy of The Metropolitan Museum of Art.)

of homes listed spinning wheels; by 1660, the number had risen to 40 percent.[76] If a loom was not present in the home, weavers in the community took the prepared yarn and wove it into cloth.[77]

As women and children were producing cloth in the home, they were also producing clothing. Once the durable cloth had been woven, the woman of the house was responsible for overseeing the cutting and stitching of the family's garments.[78] Daughters were taught the art of plain and fancy needlework at an early age. Plain needlework, comprised of simple stitches, was used to make underclothing, outer clothing, sheets, towels, and bedding for the home. Fancy needlework was part of a young girl's educational training in the skills she would need to manage her own household when the time came. One of the earliest examples of fancy needlework created by a young girl in the early colonies is the embroidery sampler completed by Loara Standish. Loara's parents, Miles and Barbara Standish, were among those who arrived on the *Mayflower.* Loara was born in 1627 and is thought to have made this sampler as a teenager while living in Duxbury, Massachusetts.[79] The sampler contains examples of the long-armed stitch, the Montenegrin cross-stitch, the double running stitch, the backstitch, the eyelet stitch, and the arrow-head stitch.[80]

INDIGENOUS TEXTILE PRODUCTION

As Indigenous women and children were funneled into Puritan homes, they too became involved in English methods of textile and clothing production.[81] While settler women spun and wove flax, cotton, and wool, Indigenous women arrived with a very different background in producing woven textiles. Indigenous women were experts in finger-weaving baskets for storing food, bags for carrying food and other portable goods, as well as strong mats used for a variety of purposes. Indigenous tightly woven mats were used to cover Wigwams, to sleep on, and to lay corn upon during harvest. Other ornamental mats were created to decorate the interior of a space and to bury the dead.[82] Women also wove belts and bracelets to be worn as accessories and for trade.[83] To create these woven pieces, Indigenous women used a variety of regional fibers in their woven textiles. Bullrush, cattail, a variety of barks, cornhusk, animal hair, wild hemp, dogbane, milkweed, wool, and nettles have been found in remnants of early Indigenous textiles in the New England area.[84] To sew woven pieces together, Indigenous women used bone needles with thread made from hemp and milkweed.[85] To the Indigenous women and children bound to service in settler homes, the English tradition of preparing and spinning flax, cotton, and wool into yarn was an unfamiliar way of creating textiles. To prepare Indigenous girls for serving in English

Figure 1.15 A 17th-century tabletop hand wheel for spinning fibers. (*17th-century spinning wheel*, wood, 370 x 280 x 530 mm (14 x 11 x 20 in), Science Museum of London. Courtesy of the Science & Society Picture Library.)

Figure 1.16 An 18th-century spinning wheel with a distaff full of linen fibers attached to the spinning wheel. (*Spinning Wheel*, 1700–1800, wood; maple, oak, 37 1/4 in. × 23 in. × 33 in (94.6 cm), gift of Mrs. Russell Sage, 1909.
Courtesy of The Metropolitan Museum of Art.)

Figure 1.17 Remnant of an American 18th-century linsey-woolsey quilted petticoat. (*Women's petticoat,* 18th century, linsey-woolsey, wool, quilted and stuffed, 33 1/2 x 102 in (85.1 x 259.1 cm). Courtesy of the Los Angeles County Museum of Art.)

Figure 1.18 Embroidery sampler finished by Loara Standish with silk thread on 50-count linen. (*Loara Standish Sampler,* 1653, linen with silk embroidery, 23 ½ x 7 ¼ in (59.6 x 18 cm). Courtesy of the Pilgrim Hall Museum.)

households, John Eliot supplied 'praying towns' with wool, cotton, spinning wheels, and instructors to teach the techniques of English textile production.[86] Instructing Indigenous women and children in the English method of producing textiles was viewed as another way to 'civilize' them.

CLOTHING

INDIGENOUS CLOTHING

According to Roger Williams in 1643, Indigenous young boys of the Northeast Narragansett people went without clothing until the age of ten or 12, while girls were covered by an apron from birth.[87] As children grew, each male and female child dressed in the gender-appropriate clothing of their culture. In the Northeast region of early America, Indigenous men were recorded wearing breechclouts, with hanging flaps both front and back. Another variation of male and female lower body wrapping was an apron, formed by tying the front and back skin flaps together at the sides of the waist. The lower body wrapping was paired with either thigh-high or knee-high leggings. Leggings were made of flat animal skins tied at several points down the outside of the legs and often held in place with garters. Indigenous women of the Northeast wore a simple knee-length wrap

Figure 1.19 Illustration of two Indigenous women wearing draped aprons with another Indigenous woman weaving a basket in the background. (*Native American Women*, 1720, engraving, 13.4 x 7.8 cm (5.2 X 3 in), *Jean Frederic Bernard*, 1720. Courtesy of the John Carter Brown Library.)

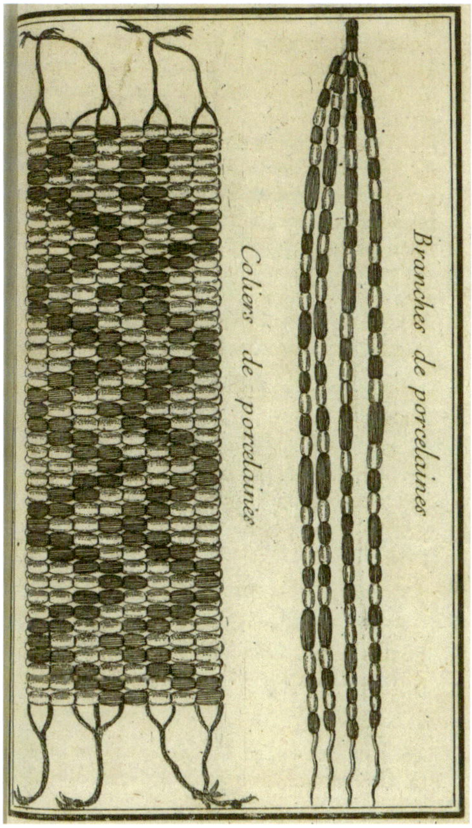

Figure 1.20 Illustration of a woven Indigenous wampum belt. (*Native American Artifacts*, 1737, engraving, 20.5 x 16.9 cm (8 x 6.6 in), *Jean Frederic Bernard*, 1737. Courtesy of the John Carter Brown Library.)

skirt of animal skins, which was held in place with a belt.[88]

In cooler weather, women added a poncho-style upper body garment. Women were also described as wearing gartered knee-length leggings that tied at the ankle.[89] In winter, men and women wore a variety of haired animal skins. In 1634, Thomas Morton described the Indigenous people of Plymouth colony wearing the hair side of the skins against their bodies in winter, and away from their bodies in summer.[90] These skin pieces came from deer, moose, beavers, otters, raccoons, wolves, and squirrels. Indigenous children wore haired animal skins in winter weather similar to the adults. Rabbit fur, in particular, was often reserved for children. John Josselyn also recorded Indigenous children wearing coats made of intricately woven turkey feathers.[91] In warmer weather, painted deer and moose skins were preferred. Writings of Roger Williams and John Josselyn both refer to warmer weather skins decorated with drawn patterns in yellow, blue, and red pigment.[92] Red ocher, yellow ocher, and a copper-rich blue clay were used to create the colorful paints that adorned the skins. These vibrant earth pigments were mixed with salmon roe, fish eggs, animal fat, oil, or bear grease to create the colorful paint paste.[93]

Sewing skins and furs together to create garments was challenging and tedious. Seventeenth-century Indigenous garments were usually based on simple construction. The shape of the clothing item relied

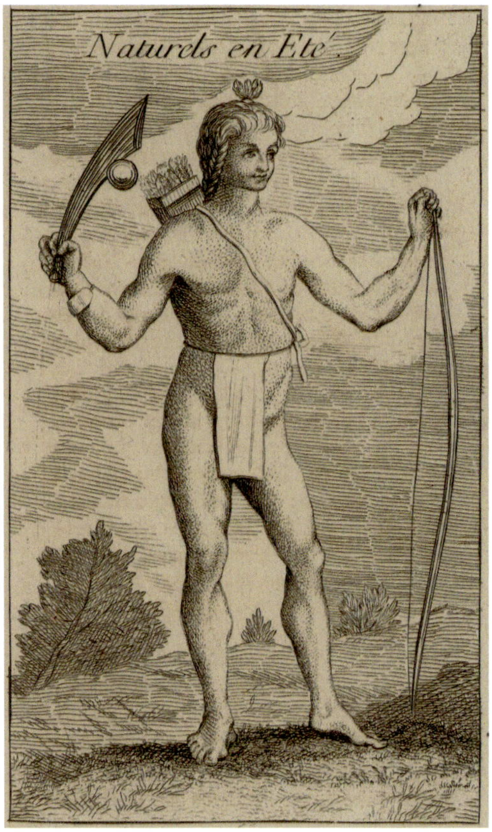

Figure 1.21 Illustration of an Indigenous man wearing a breechclout. (Le Page du Pratz, *Naturels en Ete,'* 1758, engraving, 12.7 x 7.4 (5 x 2.9 in), *Chez du Bure*, 1758. Courtesy of the John Carter Brown Library.)

on the shape of the animal from which the skin or fur was taken. Early Indigenous clothing was usually one piece held in place by ties or lacings with no seams. Simple garments could be held together with splinters of hardwood, bone, or pieces of sharp antler. In colder weather, fitting garments more closely to the body was imperative for survival in the elements. These closer-fit clothing items were created from many small pieces of skin or furs shaped more snuggly to the wearer. To sew skins and furs together, an awl made of fishbone, a hardwood splinter, or a pointed piece of bone was used to punch holes through the hides. Once the holes were created, sinew made from large tendons found in deer, moose, or elk was hand-threaded through the holes to connect the hides together, or simple sewing was done using handmade needles created from bone, wood, or ivory. Similar to modern needles, an eye was drilled at the end where sinew or plant fibers could be used as thread.[94]

With the establishment of colonial settlements, English cloth was quickly introduced to the Indigenous population for trade in the Northeast. As trade relations grew between colonists and the surrounding Indigenous people, native beaver fur was traded for a heavy blanketing that was woven 60 inches wide in deep-dyed colors. The cloth, known as duffils or trucking cloth, and was made of a coarse wool. The manufactured English cloth came in red, blue, purple, and white.[95] Red and blue seem to have been the most popular colors traded to and worn by Indigenous men, women, and children. The two-yard length of fabric was made into mantles, as well as short-sleeved coats for men, women, and children. Both the mantle and the coat could be used as blankets at night.[96] *Muckiis auhaqut* became the Narragansett term for a child's English cloth mantle.[97]

In the Southeast region surrounding Jamestown, the men of the Powhatan Confederacy wore a front drape of deerskin that tied in the back. The edges of the drape were fringed and often worn folded over the top to display two rows of fringe on the wearer. Another garment variation was a fringed lightweight skin tied on one shoulder. These draped garments were worn at times with gartered leggings, depending on the weather. Women wore a longer fringed apron that draped in front and back. An over fold of fringed skin was seen at the top of the drape to create two rows of fringe. Similar to Indigenous men, women often wore the lightweight-fringed skin tied over one shoulder.[98] These skins could also be tied around the waist with a belt made of silk grass.[99] Both men and women were also recorded wearing a type of deerskin breeches and stockings, which fastened together to protect them from bushes

Figure 1.22 Illustration of a Powhatan chief wearing a draped apron. Based on a watercolor by John White. (Theodor De Bry, *A cheiff Lorde of Roanoac*, 1590, engraving, 16.3 x 21.7 (6.4 x 8.5 in), *J. Wechel*, 1590. Courtesy of the John Carter Brown Library.)

Figure 1.23 A traditional Indigenous hand-painted deerskin parfleche. (Sioux, 1900, color pigment painted on deerskin, (Acc. No. X1996.3.5). Courtesy of the Panhandle-Plains Historical Museum.)

Figure 1.24 Illustration of an Indigenous man of Pomeiooc wearing a winter wrap made of skins. Based on a watercolor by John White. (Theodore De Bry, *An ageed manne in his winter garment*, 1590, engraving, 15.5 x 22 cm (6.1 x 8.6 in), *J. Wechel*, 1590. Courtesy of the John Carter Brown Library.)

Figure 1.25 Illustration of Powhatan people in their traditional clothing. Based on a watercolor by John White. (Theodor De Bry, *Native Americans of Virginia*, 1706, engraving, 12 x 17.2 cm (4.7 x 6.7 in), *Peiter van der Aa*, 1707. Courtesy of the John Carter Brown Library.)

Figure 1.26 An Indigenous bone awl. (Antelope Creek Phase, 1200–1500, bone, (Acc. No. A22–4H-58). Courtesy of the Panhandle-Plains Historical Museum).

Figure 1.27 An Indigenous bone needle. (Antelope Creek Phase, 1200–1500, bone, (Acc. No. A61–396). Courtesy of the Panhandle-Plains Historical Museum).

and shrubs. For warmth in winter, haired robes made of raccoon, weasel, beaver, otter, rabbit, and deerskin tied to the shoulder. In the summer, William Strachey referred to hairless deerskins of the Powhatan people embroidered with white beads and copper, or painted.[100] As for children, Powhatan boys remained without clothes until adolescence. Young girls wore a cord that tied at the waist, while another cord ran from the front of the body to the back of the body. Moss was used to cover the pubic area, which was held in place by the cord.[101] By the age of 12, girls were clothed with a leather-draped apron like their mothers. When a Powhatan boy became an adolescent, he followed the clothing tradition of his father. Both boys and girls were wrapped in skins for warmth in the winter, like their parents.[102]

ANGLO-EUROPEAN CLOTHING

From the beginning of colonization, clothing and textiles were a necessary resource and commodity. In the first shipment of colonists and supplies sent to Jamestown, six tailors were listed among the gentlemen, laborers, apothecaries, and craftsmen.[103] Clothing was used in Jamestown not only to protect individuals from the climate, but to also establish social hierarchy and position. George Percy was the most prominent man by birth among the original colonists. During his brief time in Jamestown, the amount of money Percy spent on clothing illustrates the importance clothing played in visually communicating his position in the colony. In the year 1610, Percy spent more than 58 pounds on

Figure 1.28 Illustration of Powhatan people dressed in summer and winter garments. The Powhatan person on the bottom left is wearing winter skins, while the Powhatan person on the bottom right is wearing a winter cloth mantle. (Johann Georg Purmann, *Sommer und Winter Kleider der Virginier*, 1779, engraving, 15.6 x 12.9 cm (6.1 x 5 in), *Johann Gottlieb Garb*, 1779. Courtesy of the John Carter Brown Library.)

his Jamestown wardrobe. In the same year, people of impoverished means signed binding contracts of five years of service or more for a five-pound passage to the colonies, in hopes of a better life in colonial America.[104]

The *Mayflower* also brought a tailor and a tailor's apprentice to the early colonies. Isaac Allerton, signer of the *Mayflower Compact*, worked as a tailor and brought his 12-year-old apprentice John Hooke with him on the journey.[105] In a letter to those left behind in Holland, Plymouth leader Edward Winslow advised his fellow separatists to bring a good amount of clothing with them on the journey to the colonies.[106] Later, in 1639, William Wood advised those planning to join the colony to not only bring their older and finest clothes, but to also bring cloth for trading purposes.[107] Understanding the necessity of clothing, the Massachusetts Bay Colony leaders shipped large quantities of ready-to-wear men's garments to the colonies in 1629. A provision list for the first supply ships sailing to the Massachusetts Bay Colony included 400 pairs of shoes, 300 pairs of Irish stockings, 100 pairs of knit stockings, ten dozen pairs of Norwich garters, 100 leather suits including doublets and hose, 400 falling neck bands, 100 waistcoats bound in red tape, 100 leather belts, 100 black hats, 500 red knit caps, 100 mantles, and 16 pairs of gloves.[108]

ANGLO-EUROPEAN CHILDREN'S CLOTHING

Clothing and textiles were also essential for the colonial child. In the beginning stages of life, English and European children in early New England were swaddled in bands of cloth as infants. These bands of cloth meticulously wound around the

Figure 1.29 Illustration of two Indigenous women and their toddlers in the village of Dasamonquepeuc, located a few miles outside of Roanoke Colony. Based on a watercolor by John White. (Theodor De Bry, *Their manner of careynge the Children and a tyere of the cheiffe Ladyes of the towne of Dasamonquepeuc*, 1590, engraving, 14.9 x 21 cm (5.8 x 8.2 in), *J. Wechel*, 1590. Courtesy of the John Carter Brown Library.)

Figure 1.30 Illustration of an Indigenous woman and child from the town of Pomeiooc. Based on a watercolor by John White. (Theodor De Bry, *A cheiff Layde of Pomeiooc*, 1590, engraving, 14.7 x 21.5 cm (5.7 x 8.4 in), *J.* Wechel, 1590. Courtesy of the John Carter Brown Library.)

Figure 1.31 Child's plain weave linen shirt worn by Bridge Chandler of Lexington, Massachusetts, in the third quarter of the 18th century. The scalloped ruffle at the neck and cuffs are made of a lighter-weight linen. (*Child's shirt,* 18th century, 25.1 x 58 cm (9 7/8 x 22 13/16 in), gift of Miss Ellen Stone, 1899. Courtesy of the Museum of Fine Arts, Boston.)

Figure 1.32 Child's plain weave linen shift worn by a member of the Robbins family of Lexington, Massachusetts, in the mid to late 18th century. The homespun shift has sleeve gussets and is pieced at the side. (*Child's shift,* 18th century, 67.5 x 75.5 cm (26 9/16 x 29 3/4 in), gift of Miss Ellen Stone, 1899. Courtesy of the Museum of Fine Arts, Boston.)

Figure 1.33 Homespun infant stays worn by a member of the Wood family of Duxbury, Massachusetts, in the third quarter of the 18th century. (*Infant stays*, 1775, 6 1/4 x 19 3/4 in (15.8 x 50.1 cm), gift of Cynthia Chapman Woodard, 1875. Courtesy of the Duxbury and Rural Historical Society.)

child to keep the spine and the skeletal structure protected from harm. Once an infant outgrew swaddling bands, both girls and boys were clothed in a shirt or shift with a padded corset or stays, similar to the style of their mother's. Swaddling and corseting techniques were used to ensure children grew straight and tall, as well as learned how to walk properly upright. Over the undergarments, boys and girls were placed in gowns consisting of a bodice and skirt with one or more long petticoats. Petticoats for children often had a wide waistband with a longer gathered skirt attached. To make certain a child did not crawl, but instead learned to stand and walk early, petticoats were purposefully created a foot longer than the length of the boy or girl.[109] Jackets, coats, cloaks, or mantles were added to keep children warm in cooler weather.

The layers of clothing pieces did not change for boys and girls as they learned to walk; however, the skirts and petticoats shortened to allow children the ability to walk without tripping.[110] To aid children as they learned to walk, false hanging sleeves, fabric, or ribbon ties were attached to the back of a child's bodice at the shoulders. A person assisting a child as they learned to walk held these leading strings to help the child balance. Leading strings could also be used to keep a child in close proximity.[111] An example of false hanging sleeves appears in the portrait of four-and-a-half-year-old Robert Gibbs of Boston. In the detailed painting, the unknown artist captured Robert in the dress of a boy under the age of six with hanging sleeves attached to the back of his bodice. As was customary in England and Europe, boys under the age of

Figure 1.34 Portrait of Robert Gibbs. (Freake-Gibbs painter, *Robert Gibbs at 4 1/2 Years*, 1670, oil on canvas, 101.92 x 83.82 cm (40 1/8 x 33 in), M. and M. Karolik Fund. Courtesy of the Museum of Fine Arts, Boston.)

six remained in dresses until they were well past toilet training. 'Breeching' referred to giving a boy between the ages of five and six their first pair of breeches to wear. This sometimes accompanied a celebration in early American homes, as it had in England.[112] With this transition into male clothing, young boys began to dress like their fathers in shirts, doublets, and breeches. While breeched boys no longer wore stays or a gown, girls would continue wearing these socially appropriate clothing items throughout their lifetime.

INDIGENOUS CHILDREN AND ANGLO-EUROPEAN CLOTHING

English clothing gifted to high-ranking Indigenous leaders began as a way for colony leaders to encourage Native loyalty and gain access to resources and land. English coats were also used to pay Indigenous parents for binding their children into service in English colonial homes. For those Indigenous parents who did agree, they were gifted a new English coat per year their child was in service.[113] John Eliot, in a letter to Puritan Minister Thomas Shepard, shared his goal for the Indigenous people of the first 'praying town,' Nonantum. Eliot's plan was to teach them how to build, farm, and clothe themselves like the English.[114] Differences in Indigenous dress and the lack of clothing made the English uncomfortable. Early missionary efforts placed the clothing of Indigenous men, women, and children in 'appropriate' clothing at the forefront of transitioning Native people, who they deemed as untamed, into a 'civilized' people.[115] On his visits to Nonantum, Thomas Shepard refers to many Indigenous children given to the village as well as taken

Figure 1.35 Illustration of Indigenous women and children in European-influenced clothing. (Bacqueville de La Potherie, *Native American mothers and children*, 1723, engraving, 13.1 x 16.3 (5.1 x 6.4 in), *Henry des Bordes*, 1723. Courtesy of the John Carter Brown Library.)

to be educated and raised in the English tradition. These 'praying town' children were clothed in English-style garments and given English-style haircuts. Shepard also recorded, on a later visit to Nonatum, his pleased reaction to seeing so many Indigenous men, women, and children dressed in English clothing. According to his documents, English-style clothing had been gifted to the Indigenous inhabitants of Nonantum or made by the Indigenous people themselves.[116] Clothing Indigenous children in English-style garments made binding them into Puritan households as servants an easier transition for both the leaders of 'praying towns' and the Puritan population.

Children of early 17th century America were surrounded by challenging political and social complexities. Depending upon their cultural background and the status of their birth parents, as designated by the English system of government, children experienced vast differences in the lives they were assigned. Often, the lives to which children were appointed focused on the labor they could provide for English and European family units as well as the new communities they were connected to. With early textile and clothing production taking place in the home and at the community level, involving children from all backgrounds in the creation of these necessary staples, made it possible for expanding colonial settlements to work toward becoming more self-sufficient. This allowed for the customary textile and clothing practices of Anglo-European colonists to take root in early America.

NOTES

1 Ann Marie Plane, *Colonial Intimacies: Indian Marriage in Early New England* (Ithaca: Cornell University Press, 2000), 65.
2 Kathleen J. Bragdon, *Native People of Southern New England: 1500 to 1650* (Norman: University of Oklahoma Press, 1996), 18–19.
3 Plane, *Colonial Intimacies*, 5.
4 Stephen M. Sachs, "Remembering the Traditional Meaning and Role of Kinship in American Indian Societies, To Overcome Problems of Favoritism in Contemporary Tribal Government," *Indigenous Policy* 22, no. 2 (Fall 2011): 1, 5.
5 Jenny Hale Pulsipher, *Subjects unto the Same King: Indians, English, and the Context for Authority in Colonial New England* (Philadelphia: University of Pennsylvania Press, 2005), 13; Bragdon, *Native People: 1500 to 1650*, 24.
6 Bragdon, 102–18.
7 Leo Kevin Killsback, "A Nation of Families: Traditional Kinship, the Foundation for Cheyenne Sovereignty," *AlterNative* 15, no. 1 (2019): 36.
8 Bragdon, 169.
9 Timothy R. Pauketat, "Refiguring the Archaeology of Greater Cahokia," *Journal of Archaeological Research* 6, no. 1 (1998): 59, 60, www.jstor.org/stable/41053152.
10 Richard Middleton and Anne Lombard, *Colonial America: A History to 1763*, 4th ed. (West Sussex: Wiley-Blackwell, 2011), 19.
11 Bragdon, 145; Ida M. Wrightman, *The Mayhew Manor of Tisby: Address Prepared for the New York Branch of the Order of Colonial Lords of Manors in America* (London: FB & C, 2016), 7, Google Books.
12 Christopher J. Bilodeau, "The Paradox of Sagadahoc: The Popham Colony, 1607–1608," *Early American Studies* 12, no. 1 (2014): 4–11, www.jstor.org/stable/24474845.
13 William Bradford, *History of Plimoth Plantation* (Carlisle, MA: Applewood Books, 2010), 8.
14 Alan Greer, *Property and Dispossession: Natives, Empires, and Land in Early Modern North America*, ed. Frederick Hoxie et al. (New York: Cambridge University Press, 2018), 88.
15 David Hackett Fischer, *Albion's Seed: Four British Folkways in America* (New York: Oxford University Press, 1989), 16.
16 Greer, *Property and Dispossession*, 88, 201–8, 228.
17 Fischer, *Albion's Seed*, 16; Greer, 203.
18 Bilodeau, "The Paradox of Sagadahoc," 5–8, 23–25; Lawrence Stone, "Social Mobility in England, 1500–1700," *Past & Present*, no. 33 (1966): 18, www.jstor.org/stable/649801.
19 Stone, "Social Mobility in England," 18.
20 Mary Newton Standard, *Colonial Virginia Its People and Customs* (Philadelphia: J. B. Lippincott Company, 1917), 16, Google Books.
21 Margaret Ellen Newell, *Brethren by Nature: New England Indians, Colonists, and the Origins of American Slavery* (Ithaca: Cornell University Press, 2015), 44.
22 "Poor Children to Be Sent to Virginia," *The Virginia Magazine of History and Biography* 6, no. 3 (January 1899): 232, www.jstor.org/stable/4242155.
23 "Poor Children to Be Sent," 232.
24 Ruth Wallis Herndon and John E. Murray, eds., *Children Bound to Labor: The Pauper Apprentice System in Early America* (Ithaca: Cornell University Press, 2009), 29.
25 John Demos, *A Little Commonwealth: Family Life in Plymouth Colony*, 2nd ed. (Oxford: Oxford University Press, 2000), 71.
26 Peter Kolchin, *American Slavery 1619–1877* (New York: Hill and Wang, 2003), 11.
27 Joyce E. Chaplin, "Food and the Material Origins of Early America," in *Food in Time and Place: The American Historical Association Companion to Food History*, ed. Paul Freedman, Joyce E. Chaplin, and Ken Albala, 1st ed. (University of California Press, 2014), 149–51, www.jstor.org/stable/10.1525/j.ctt7zw3tn.13.
28 Middleton and Lombard, *Colonial America*, 97; Newell, *Brethren by Nature*, 69.
29 Michael L. Fickes, "'They Could Not Endure That Yoke': The Captivity of Pequot Women and Children after the War of 1637," *The New England Quarterly* 73, no. 1 (2000): 78, https://doi.org/10.2307/366745.
30 Newell, 89.
31 Norman Earl Tanis, "Education in John Eliot's Indian Utopias, 1646–1675," *History of Education Quarterly* 10, no. 3 (1970): 316, https://doi.org/10.2307/367526.
32 Plane, 65.
33 Plane, 34.
34 Tanis, "Education in John Eliot's Indian Utopias," 313.
35 John Eliot and Kenneth M. Morrison, "'That Art of Coyning Christians: John Eliot and the Praying Indians of Massachusetts," *Ethnohistory* 21, no. 1 (1974): 89–90, https://doi.org/10.2307/481131.
36 Kolchin, *American Slavery*, 10–13.
37 Newell, 44; Kolchin, 6–8.

38 James Kendall Hosmer, ed., *Winthrop's Journal, "History of New England," 1630–1649* (New York: Charles Scribner's Sons, 1908), 7, 227, 228, 260, Google Books.
39 Newell, 44; Kolchin, 6–8.
40 Bernard Rosenthal, "Puritan Conscience and New England Slavery," *The New England Quarterly* 46, no. 1 (1973): 65, https://doi.org/10.2307/364886.
41 Gloria McCahon Whiting, "Race, Slavery, and the Problem of Numbers in Early New England: A View from Probate Court," *The William and Mary Quarterly* 77, no. 3 (2020): 430–34, www.jstor.org/stable/10.5309/willmaryquar.77.3.0405.
42 Rosenthal, "Puritan Conscience," 65.
43 Whiting, "Race, Slavery, and the Problem of Numbers," 430–34.
44 George Francis Dow, *Every Day Life in the Massachusetts Bay Colony* (New York: Dover Publications, 1988), 101.
45 Demos, *A Little Commonwealth*, 62, 64.
46 Edmund S. Morgan, *The Puritan Family: Religion and Domestic Relations in Seventeenth-Century New England* (Mansfield Centre: Martino Publishing, 2014), 9, 19, 28.
47 Morgan, *The Puritan Family*, 28, 29.
48 Demos, 142.
49 Morgan, 28, 29.
50 Dow, *Every Day Life*, 63.
51 Tanis, 317.
52 James Marten, ed., *Children in Colonial America* (New York: New York University Press, 2007), 33, 40, 41; Newell, 90.
53 Calvin B. Coulter, "The Import Trade of Colonial Virginia," *The William and Mary Quarterly* 2, no. 3 (1945): 296, https://doi.org/10.2307/1921454.
54 *Probate Inventory of Mary Ring* (Plymouth: Plymouth County Registry of Deeds, 1631), 1–4.
55 Dow, 242.
56 Susan M. Ouellette, *Us Textile Production in Historical Perspective: A Case Study from Massachusetts* (New York: Routledge; Taylor and Francis Group, 2012), 5.
57 Marten, *Children in Colonial America*, 128.
58 Demos, 142.
59 Ouellette, *Us Textile Production in Historical Perspective*, 45.
60 William R. Bagnall, *The Textile Industries of the United States*, vol. 1 (Cambridge: Riverside Press, 1893), 3, Google Books.
61 Kathleen A. Staples and Madelyn Shaw, *Clothing Through American History* (Oxford: Greenwood, 2013), 143.
62 Bagnall, *Textile Industries of the United States*, 3–5.
63 Ouellette, 7.
64 Ouellette, 12.
65 Bagnall, 7, 8.
66 Standard, *Colonial Virginia*, 55.
67 Herndon and Murray, *Children Bound to Labor*, 23; Edith Abbott, "A Study of the Early History of Child Labor in America," *American Journal of Sociology* 14, no. 1 (1908): 20, www.jstor.org/stable/2762758.
68 *New England's First Fruits: With Divers other Special Matters Concerning that Country* (London: R. O. and G. D. for Henry Overton, 1643), 39.
69 Laurel Thatcher Ulrich, *The Age of Homespun: Objects and Stories in the Creation of an American Myth* (New York: Vintage Books, 2001), 51.
70 Staples and Shaw, *Clothing Through American History*, 106.
71 S. G. Stephens, "The Origin of Sea Island Cotton," *Agricultural History* 50, no. 2 (1976): 394–95, www.jstor.org/stable/3741338.
72 *New England's First Fruits*, 39.
73 Dow, 94.
74 Ouellette, 35; Cecil Lubell, ed., *Textile Collections of the World: Volume 1 United States and Canada* (New York: Van Nostrand Reinhold Company, 1976), 131.
75 Dow, 94–95.
76 Ulrich, *The Age of Homespun*, 84.
77 Dow, 94.
78 Dow, 94.
79 Susan Burrows Swan, *Plain & Fancy: American Women and Their Needlework, 1700–1850* (New York: Routledge, 1977), 12–13.
80 "Loara Standish Sampler," *Textile Research Center: Leiden*, January 24, 2017, https://trc-leiden.nl/trc-needles/individual-textiles-and-textile-types/samplers/loara-standish-sampler.
81 Newell, 73.
82 Bragdon, 114; Ulrich, 45.
83 Bragdon, 97, 112.
84 Ulrich, 46–48.
85 Newell, 76.
86 Stephens, "The Origin of Sea Island Cotton," 214; Tanis, 317.
87 Roger Williams, *A Key to the Language of America* (Bedford: Applewood Books, 1936), 118–20, Google Books.
88 Carl Waldman, *Encyclopedia of Native American Tribes*, 3rd ed. (New York: Checkmark Books, 2006), 13; Josephine Paterek, *Encyclopedia of American Indian Costume* (New York: W.W. Norton & Company, 1993), 42.

89 Paterek, *American Indian Costume*, 42.

90 Thomas Morton, *New English Caanan of Thomas Morton* (New York: Burt Franklin, 1883), 142, Google Books.

91 John Josselyn, *An Account of Two Voyages to New England Made the Years 1638, 1663* (Boston: William Veazie, 1674), 111, Google Books.

92 Williams, *A Key to the Language*, 120; Josselyn, *An Account of Two Voyages*, 100.

93 Paterek, 449.

94 Paterek, 434.

95 Bragdon, 134.

96 Ulrich, 55.

97 Williams, 120; Josselyn, 101.

98 Paterek, 22.

99 Edward Wright Haile, ed., *Jamestown Narratives: Eyewitness Accounts of the Virginia Colony, the First Decade, 1607–1617* (Champlain, VA: RoundHouse, 1998), 633.

100 Haile, *Jamestown Narratives*, 630.

101 Paterek, 22.

102 Haile, 631.

103 Haile, 253.

104 Michael A. Lacombe, "'A Continuall and Dayly Table for Gentlemen of Fashion': Humanism, Food, and Authority at Jamestown, 1607–1609," *The American Historical Review* 115, no. 3 (2010): 667, www.jstor.org/stable/23302942.

105 Marten, 130.

106 Edward Winslow, "Certain Useful Directions for Such as Intend a Voyage into Those Parts," in *Mourt's Relation or Journal of the Plantation at Plymouth* (London: John Bellamie, 1622), Internet Archive.

107 William Wood, *New England's Prospect* (London: John Dawson, 1639), 42–47, University of North Dakota Scholarly Commons.

108 Nathan B. Shurtleff, ed., *Records of the Governor and Company of the Massachusetts Bay in New England 1628–1641* (Boston: William White, Printer to the Commonwealth, 1854), 1, 23–25.

109 Karen Calvert, *Children in the House: The Material Culture of Early Childhood, 1600–1900* (Boston: Northeastern University Press, 1992), 21–22.

110 Calvert, *Children in the House*, 31–33; Staples and Shaw, 371, 381, 382.

111 Demos, 140; Estelle Ansley Worrell, *Children's Costume in America 1607–1910* (New York: Charles Scribner's Sons, 1980), 9.

112 Worrell, *Children's Costume in America*, 9.

113 Ulrich, 58.

114 Thomas Shepard, *The Clear Sunshine of the Gospel Breaking Forth Upon the Indians in New-England* (London: R. Cotes for Bellamy, 1648), 59.

115 Bragdon, 19.

116 Shepard, *The Clear Sunshine*, 34, 49, 49.

CHAPTER TWO

1660–1700

With the expansion of the colonies and the need for more physical labor, early government systems found ways in the mid to late 17th century to funnel children into the workforce on a large scale. The social structure of Anglo-European homes expected children to become contributing members of the household and the community by the age of seven.[1] This philosophy extended to poor, orphaned, and indentured Anglo-European children as well as Indigenous, African, and mixed-race children. As the need for labor grew, Anglo-European settlers began to partner with Indigenous slave traders who fed the transatlantic slave trade system with Indigenous prisoners that could be sold for profit and needed commodities.[2] In many instances, Indigenous women and children were the most sought-after captives for trade.[3] Wealthy plantation owners connected to the Indigenous slave trade could purchase numerous African slaves as well as needed supplies for their growing plantations. The more slaves a plantation owner possessed, the more land he could acquire from the English government.[4]

Increased involvement in the slave trade quickly shifted the burden of heavy labor away from indentured servants and poor children to Indigenous slavery, which then led to African and mixed-race slavery.[5] As colonial settlements and plantations expanded, so did the need for textiles. This growing need led colonists to become focused on and dedicated to producing their own textiles for their everyday needs. Children of all economic and cultural backgrounds were involved in textile and clothing production. Specific tasks related to textile and clothing production in the home and in the community were assigned according to gender.[6] Not surprisingly, fabrics and clothing styles for children were linked to social status. Clothing for Upper-class children was comprised of several layers of expensive imported fabrics, while poor and enslaved children possessed little to no homespun clothing items. This chapter will focus on New England, Virginia, Maryland, and the Carolinas in relation to child labor, colonial textile production, and clothing practices dependent upon the social status of a child.

COMMUNITIES: SOCIAL AND POLITICAL STRUCTURE

NEW ENGLAND COMMUNITIES

With the year 1660 came the restoration of the English monarchy and the return of the House of Stuart. During the reign of Charles II, Dutch New

DOI: 10.4324/9781003230441-3

Figure 2.1 Map detailing the English colonies and Indigenous communities in 1685. (Christopher Browne, publisher, *A new map of Virginia, Maryland, and the improved parts of Pennsylvania & New Jersey*, 1685, 48 x 55 cm (London: Christopher Browne 1685), Library of Congress.)

Netherland was overtaken by English rule, which added the colonies of New York and New Jersey to the empire.[7] By 1665, over 80 English towns dotted the New England landscape with an estimated 50,000 colonists, in contrast to the 10,000 to 15,000 Indigenous people inhabiting the surrounding area.[8] A majority of these New England towns were comprised of Puritan family households.[9]

Child labor and education were fused together in early New England.[10] Between the ages of five and seven, children were expected to begin contributing to the family or the community. Girls were instructed to learn domestic skills, including textile production, as future wives and mothers in the colony. Having females in the home who could spin yarn and produce textiles was an economic benefit to any household. Boys were expected to learn a lawful trade for future employment to support their own family as an adult.[11] Puritans felt children learned more effectively when their parents did not teach them. For this reason, Puritan parents 'put out' or 'sent out' their children to another family to learn these necessary skills. This seemed to be the case in both lower-income and higher-income families.[12]

Anglo-European Poor Children

A common practice in New England was to place poor children in homes of masters who would teach them a skill or trade. This pauper apprenticeship system was born out of a series of English laws beginning in 1536, which bound poor children to a male master, often involuntarily.[13] The appointed master was expected to educate and train the child,

Figure 2.2 Illustration of a Puritan couple. (George Henry Boughton, *Puritans going to church*, 1884, illustration, Library of Congress.)

Figure 2.3 The Conant House in Watertown, Massachusetts, constructed in the late 17th century. (Historic American Buildings Survey, *Conant House, Watertown, Middlesex County, MA*, 1933, photograph, Library of Congress.)

as well as raise the pauper apprentice to become a useful and hardworking member of the community. The ages of bound-out children could be as young as three through to the mid-teen years. Boys were indentured until the age of 21, while girls were indentured until the age of 18.[14] By the turn of the 18th century, thousands of destitute and abandoned children moved through the pauper apprenticeship system of the early American colonies.[15]

Community officials also used servitude and pauper apprenticeships as a way to rebuild household productivity when a home was lacking efficiency. The family labor system in New England was important for self-sufficiency and keeping members of the colony from needing poor relief. To assist with family labor shortages, placing orphans and poor children in homes was widely practiced.[16] As colonies grew, additional structures were put in place to handle the expanding number of poor children. Boston established the Overseers of the Poor in the late 17th century to apprentice destitute children in a home or employment that could benefit the child and the community at large.[17] These poor and orphaned New England children became young laborers harnessed for economic stability and often textile production.[18]

Indigenous Children

As colonial leaders learned from the Pequot War, using Indigenous labor as well as trading Indigenous people for African labor on the transatlantic slave trade system had its benefits.[19] Indigenous men, women, and children who were not traded in the transatlantic slave network were kept in the

Figure 2.4 Historic marker for the praying town of Hassanamesit established in 1651. (Doug Kerr, *Grafton, Massachusetts*, 2010, photograph, Wikipedia Commons.)

colony as labor.[20] In addition, New England 'praying towns' continued to provide a steady source of Indigenous children for placement in English homes as indentured servants. English leaders of 'praying towns' recommended the placement of as many Indigenous children as possible in English homes, with the consent of the children's parents. The ideal outcome for these 'praying town' leaders was to see Indigenous boys learn a trade, while Indigenous girls learned appropriate English domestic skills, which included textile production.[21]

Many more Indigenous children were bound as servants after King Philip's War ended in 1676.[22] Males over the age of 14 were sold into slavery in the West Indies, as well as some of their wives. Women who were not sold into slavery, along with children, were bound as servants to English colonists who served in the war.[23] In Plymouth, Rhode Island, and Massachusetts, courts decided where these women and children were placed and how long they would serve. Terms of service for these captives ranged from as little as five years to as long as a lifetime. By the turn of the 18th century, historians estimate 1,000 Indigenous people were enslaved or bound to English colonists in Rhode Island, Massachusetts, and Connecticut.[24]

African Children

While the documented number of enslaved Africans in New England was low in the early 17th century, in the last quarter of the 17th century and the first half of the 18th century, the number rose.[25] Merchants from Boston, New London, Newport, and Bristol chartered ships to Africa where they traded goods for captured African men, women, and children.[26] Influential merchant class families

Figure 2.5 Portrait of King Philip, sachem of the Wampanoags. (Benjamin Church, *King Philip*, 1675, engraving, 12.2 X 7.9 cm (4.8 x 3.1 in). Courtesy of John Carter Brown Library.)

in the Massachusetts Bay and Rhode Island colonies used growing participation in the African slave trade as profit to invest in industrial growth.[27] Two merchant class families, the Cabots of Massachusetts and the Browns of Rhode Island, transferred their wealth and association with the transatlantic slave trade down through their family lines. By the end of the 18th century, the descendants of the Cabots and the Browns invested in and laid the foundation for the creation of the American textile industry.[28]

Although the slave trade initially began in Massachusetts, Rhode Island soon dominated the trade in New England. Over time, Rhode Island owned 523 slaving ships, which carried slaves to 40 world slave posts, including posts in the colonies.[29] By the 1690s, African men, women, and children made up 87 percent of the bound labor in New England as the percentage of European and Indigenous labor decreased.[30] African slavery was used for plantation work in southern New England, while the northern colonies used African labor in the home, in industry and in shipping.[31] New England's focused involvement in the African slave trade by the turn of the 18th century shifted bondage for life away from Indigenous men, women, and children to solely Black slavery.[32] As the need for African labor rose in the southern colony plantation system, New Englanders became slave traders while southern planters became slaveholders.[33]

VIRGINIA AND MARYLAND COMMUNITIES

Historians have linked Sir William Berkeley, appointed governor of Virginia, to the societal structure of colonial Virginia.[34] Berkeley actively recruited English Royalist families from southwest England to relocate to Virginia between 1647 and 1660.[35] Along with their social hierarchy traditions, Virginia's elite also brought the agricultural plantation system, which thrived on a history of domestic bondage and slavery.[36] As time progressed in colonial Virginia, large estates with sizable tracts of land for agricultural development required substantial labor. Supplying labor to these plantations became the focus for Virginia planters. This British-style plantation system relied on indentured servant labor first, continued with poor Virginian children, moved to Indigenous slavery, and then shifted completely to African slavery.[37]

Maryland also had a man of ambition and means as the propelling force behind its colonization. George Calvert, the first Lord Baltimore, persuaded Charles I to gift him a territory in the colonies that would solely be under Calvert's authority. Lord Baltimore's primary goal was to increase his estates as well as elevate his family's position among

Figure 2.6 Illustration of a West Indies sugar plantation in 1667. (Sebastien Le Clerc, *Sucrerie*, 1667, engraving, 20.2 x 34.5 cm (7.9 x 13.5 in). Courtesy of the John Carter Brown Library.)

Figure 2.7 Image of Shirley plantation built on Weynoke land in Virginia. Colonel Edward Hill was granted the land in 1660. (Francas Benjamin Johnston, Historic American Buildings Survey, *Shirley, Charles City County, Virginia*, 1932, photograph, 8 x 10 in (20.32 x 25.4 cm), Library of Congress.)

English noblemen. Maryland was first settled in 1634 by 25 English gentlemen under the leadership of Lord Baltimore's sons. Each member of the gentry was given large tracts of land depending on the number of servants they brought with them.[38] In contrast to other colonial settlements, Maryland did not attract families in its early years.[39]

Anglo-European Poor Children

In an effort to bring more children into the labor force of colonial Virginia, lawmakers adopted the British system of binding out poor children into servitude.[40] Like New England, children in this system were often abandoned, illegitimate, taken from neglectful parents, or parents who could not financially support their families.[41] If a child had no parents or family, town officials auctioned them to bidders who needed additional labor. Most often, the highest bidders were plantation owners.[42] According to scholars, tens of thousands of poor Anglo-European children were bound out for labor in colonial Virginia.[43] Pauper apprenticeship became a Virginia welfare policy for English and European children, which tapped into and controlled child labor.[44]

In contrast to Virginia, Maryland experienced a large number of orphan children in the 17th century.[45] This was due to the reality of mid-life mortality and later-in-life marriages in the colony. Twenty percent of all Maryland children were orphaned by the age of 12.[46] To address this community challenge, a system of apprenticing orphans was created by Maryland officials. The established

Figure 2.8 Image of Indian Banks Plantation constructed on the site of a Moraughtacund Indigenous village visited by John Smith in 1608. The plantation was initially constructed in 1699. (Robert Gamble, Charles E. Peterson, and John O Brostrip, Historic American Buildings Survey, *Indian Banks, State Route 606, Tidewater, Richmond, VA,* 1933 photograph, Library of Congress.)

system oversaw estate dealings for wealthy orphan children and simultaneously bound out poorer children into service. Children of moderate means were placed in craft training and educational contracts with employers, while manual labor was reserved for poor and illegitimate children.[47]

Indigenous Children

In addition to English indentured servants and child labor, the Indigenous slave trade found its way to Virginia by 1650.[48] Virginia traders encountered and established trade relations with an armed group of Erie tribesmen who were heavily involved in the commercial Indigenous slave trade. These Erie Indigenous slavers, later known as the Westo, remained based in Virginia until 1674 when their raids for Indigenous captives extended further south into the Carolinas, Spanish Florida, and Georgia.[49] As a result of Bacon's Rebellion in 1676, the Indigenous slave trade accelerated. Indigenous children provided the highest percentage of slave labor in Henrico County, Virginia, which was the center of the Indigenous slave trade along the James River.[50] Like Virginia, Maryland also holds an early history of Indigenous slavery. In 1639, legislature recognized the practice of both Indigenous and African slavery within its social and economic structure. The combination of Indigenous and African slavery existed until the 1660s when the transition to primarily African slavery began.[51]

African and Mixed-Race Children

As the need for labor increased in the 1680s due to expanding plantations in Virginia and Maryland, the number of English and European immigrants arriving as indentured servants began to decline

Figure 2.9 Map detailing the location of all English plantations, including those in North America. (Robert Morden, *A New Map of the English Plantations in America, both Continent and Islands, Shewing their true Situation and distance from England or one with another*, 1673, engraving, 43.7 x 54 cm (17.2 x 21.2 in). Courtesy of the John Carter Brown Library.)

and continued to decrease.[52] This coincided with the increase of availability of African slave labor with the establishment of the British Royal African Company in 1672.[53] In 1698, Parliament fueled the increase of African slave trading by opening the trade to all English citizens with the African Trade Act. This change expanded the trade of African slaves exponentially.[54] Plantation owners could not only purchase slave labor more cheaply, but unlike indentured servants, slaves were bound to their masters for life. African slaves were also from a foreign land and therefore less likely to escape, in contrast to local Indigenous slaves.[55]

Slave laws passed in both Virginia and Maryland by Upper-class English plantation owners, merchants, and professionals, made it easy for African slave owners to multiply their labor investment over time, particularly in the case of children. By 1630, mixed-race children of Anglo-European and African descent were being born in the colonies. In an effort to classify children of mixed race as lower than children of pure Anglo-European descent, Virginia lawmakers passed a significant slave code in 1662. Regardless of the lineage of the father, all children born of African women remained slaves for life. In Maryland, children born of Anglo-European women and African men were bound to a lifetime of slavery, as their fathers were, beginning in 1664. Any mixed-race children born before 1664 were bound for 30 years of service.[56] As the need for plantation labor increased in the 1690s and 1700s, Upper-class planters, who served in legislative positions, created legal structures that continued to enslave certain mixed-race children while placing others in indentured service.[57]

CAROLINA COMMUNITIES

By 1660, plantation owners in the West Indies began looking for additional land to expand their economic enterprise. Sir John Colleton, a wealthy English plantation owner in Barbados, was the catalyst for the establishment of the Carolinas.[58] Colleton, along with Governor William Berkeley of Virginia, formed an alliance with six other influential and powerful English noblemen to obtain the Carolina Charter from Charles II in 1663.[59] By 1669, the proprietors approved the creation of the Fundamental Constitution of the Carolinas, which included the acceptance of Black slavery by granting every free male settler absolute power over his African slaves.[60] The 'head right' system of granting land further encouraged slavery by gifting each head of household 20 acres of land per African male slave and ten acres of land for each female slave.[61]

INDIGENOUS AND AFRICAN POPULATION

The Native population in the Carolina region was substantially larger than the population of the Chesapeake Bay region of Virginia and Maryland. Thousands of Indigenous men, women, and children surrounded each small English settlement. The coastal Native inhabitants of South Carolina, known as 'Settlement Indians,' were among the first Indigenous people to encounter the Carolina colonists.[62] Early colonists interacted with the South Carolina coastal people as well as the Kusso, Stuno, Esaw, Westo, Waniah, and Savannah people in varying degrees.[63] The early colonies of Carolina heavily relied on the Indigenous population for their survival. The surrounding Indigenous population fed the colonists, exchanged quality Native goods the English could trade for profit, and protected them from external threats.[64]

As planters and merchants established themselves in South Carolina, the need for labor and economic profit increased. The colonists' need for plantation supplies and labor connected to capital gain outweighed the wishes of the proprietors to keep peace with the neighboring Indigenous populations. Early South Carolina merchants also needed

Figure 2.10 Image of plantation house owned by Colonel William Rhett, initial construction 1700, Charleston, South Carolina. (Historic American Buildings Survey, *Colonel William Rhett House, 54 Hasell Street, Charleston, SC*, 1933, photograph, Library of Congress.)

to find a means for profit. Two highly prized commodities, which sold easily on the transatlantic trade system, were human labor and deerskins.[65] Carolina leaders soon made an alliance with the Westo, which provided high-profit returns from the Indigenous slave trade. Selling Indigenous men, women, and children along with deerskins on a large scale, in alliance with the Westo, provided Carolina plantation owners and merchants with supplies, African labor, horses, livestock, and a growing economy.[66]

As the relationship with the Westo became less profitable, colony leadership formed alliances with the nearby Savannah tribe to overtake the Westo. The Savannah people, who had not been slave traders previously, were coerced into capturing Westo and Wahiah people to continue the profitable Indigenous slave trade. Carolina officials and profit-minded leaders knew continuation of the slave trade was necessary to sustain Carolina's economy.[67] Between 1675 and 1715, an estimated 30,000 to 50,0000 captive Indigenous men, women, and children were exported as slaves through Charles Town Harbor.[68] The most sought-after Indigenous slaves on the transatlantic slave trade system were women and children. Children, in particular, were easier to control, learned other languages and work skills quickly, while serving their masters for life.[69]

At the same time as thousands of Indigenous people were being exported and sold into slavery, African slavery was expanding in the Carolinas. In 1695, there were 2,000 African slaves accounted

Figure 2.11 Illustration of two Indigenous women and two infants with another child strapped to a cradleboard hanging from a tree. (Thomas Lombrail, *Two Native American women with babies; child on cradleboard*, 1707, engraving, 13.4 x 7.7 cm (5.27 x 3 in). Courtesy of the John Carter Brown Library.)

for; by 1708, African slaves had become the majority population in South Carolina.[70] As the population increased, so did fears of slave rebellion against the minority of Anglo-European plantation owners. Stories of rebellion in Barbados, Antigua, and Jamaica propelled the creation of extreme slave laws in the later 17th century. Slave laws were put into place as early as 1683. By 1696, South Carolina slave codes called, "*The Act for the Better Ordering of Slaves,*" became the most punitive in the English colonies.[71] Among the slave codes of 1696, children of African, Mulatto, or Indian descent bought or sold within South Carolina remained slaves for life, as did their parents.[72]

TEXTILES AND TEXTILE PRODUCTION

With colonial expansion, the need for larger quantities of textiles for everyday living also increased. New England probate records from the 17th century highlight how essential cloth was to the early American home. Fabric yardages needed to create necessary clothing for each adult ranged between 40 and 50 yards per year. With an estimated population of 50,000 colonists by 1665, New England settlers alone would have needed well over a million yards of ready-made fabric in one year to clothe the men, women, and children in their communities.[73] Between 1651 and 1673, in order to cut off trade between the colonies and other countries, Parliament passed a series of Navigation Acts which affected the colonists and who they bought textiles from.[74]

Colonists could no longer buy less expensive textiles from other countries. Textiles could only be purchased from English merchant ships, even if the textiles were originally created in other countries. Additionally, colonists could only export their goods through English ships. With each transaction, colonists were charged additional taxes and duties attached to textiles coming in and textile materials going out of the colony. The Navigation Act of 1673 limited trade further by attaching these same duties and taxes to items that were shipped between English colonies.[75] Relying solely on imported textiles for clothing was not economically realistic for the colonial family. The need for more locally made textiles to clothe settlers and their families led to an increase in the types of textiles created in the colonies, as well as the development of a more organized system of cloth production in the home and in the community. By the end of the 17th century, three-quarters of the textiles needed in the New England home were locally made.[76]

TEXTILE PRODUCTION IN THE COLONIES

In addition to flax, hemp, and cotton used for homespun textiles, the expansion of raising sheep in early America led to a large quantity of locally made wool cloth in homes and in the community. Spun wool by itself could be used to produce knitted garments or fabric. Sheep could provide both woolen and worsted textiles. Woolen yarn was created from short spun fibers, while worsted yarn was created from longer and finer fibers. Woolen textiles were known for their fuzzy texture. Worsted textiles could be combed or pressed to create a smooth surface.[77] The most common types of wool cloth woven in the colonies were broadcloth, serge, and kersey. Broadcloth was the most expensive to produce, due to the detailed finishing techniques used to create the fabric. Broadcloth was created from worsted yarn, often dyed, and processed at a fulling mill to produce a felted fabric that was thick, textured, and warm. Serge was a mid-weight twill weave fabric finished by a less in-depth process. Kersey was the least expensive wool cloth produced in the colonies. Kersey consisted of a twill weave created from the roughest yarn and not fulled or finished. Due to the lack of finishing used to complete the cloth, Kersey was sold cheaply in the colonies and often worn by lower-income families or the poor.[78]

From the completion of the first fulling mill in Rowley, Massachusetts, in 1643, to the late 17th century, the amount of woolen cloth finished at the mill rose dramatically as colonial textile production increased. Between the years 1672 and 1688, an estimated 100,000 yards of woolen cloth were finished at the fulling mill.[79] This estimate does not include the linen, linen and cotton blended 'mixed cloths,' or linsey-woolsey textiles produced in the area during that time.[80] News of textile production in the colonies traveled back to England. In order to offset the production of homespun cloth, Parliament banned the export of textile manufacturing equipment to the colonies in 1695. This challenge

Figure 2.12 Illustration of sheep owned by a settler in early 18th-century North America. (Claude-Charles LeRoy, *Sheep Grazing on Settler's Roof*, 1722, engraving, 13 x 7.7 cm (5 x 3 in). Courtesy of the John Carter Brown Library.)

from England did not impede manufacturing; in fact, just the opposite occurred. In 1698, New England merchants began exporting the surplus yardage of finished woolen textiles for profit. In an effort to stop the colonies from trading finished textile goods for economic gain, Parliament passed an additional law in 1699 stating that no wool, wool yarn, wool cloth, or wool clothing from the American colonies could be loaded on board any ship or vessel for trade purposes. The colonies were also forbidden to trade woolen goods with other established English colonies.[81] The colonists producing textiles were becoming independent, industrious, and in direct commercial competition with England.

New England was not the only colony producing large amounts of textiles in homes and communities. Virginia began organizing steps in 1662

Figure 2.13 Image of the Stony Brook Mill located in Brewster, Massachusetts. This location housed one of the first fulling mills, built in 1664. The fulling mill burned in 1760 and was replaced by a woolen mill. (Historic American Buildings Survey, *Stony Brook Mill, Old Coach Road, Brewster, Barnstable County, MA*, 1933, photograph, Library of Congress.)

for cloth production on a sizable scale.[82] The Navigation Acts greatly affected the tobacco trade for smaller-scale farmers in Virginia who made a profit from growing and selling their tobacco. The trade restrictions of the Navigation Acts caused an economic depression. Where once there was a surplus for the Virginia farmer, now there was poverty. Families could not afford the high prices of imported cloth or clothing. Small farms and larger plantations in Virginia turned to creating their own textiles.[83] To increase the production of textiles, commissioners of each county in Virginia were instructed to build houses for the education of poor children in the art of spinning and weaving in 1668.[84]

Documented textile production was also occurring in New York, New Jersey, and Pennsylvania in the late 17th century. Daniel Denton, a colonial writer and observer of life in New York and New Jersey, recorded in 1670 that most Dutch homes in New York produced their own linen and a percentage of wool cloth for their everyday clothing. Flax and wool fibers from New York farms were spun and woven in the homes of productive colonists. West Jersey was also reported to produce several types of woolen cloth as well as linen in 1697. Soon after Philadelphia was founded in 1682, many German families with textile production skills settled in the area. In a short period of time, immigrant families of Pennsylvania built a reputation for producing fine linen yarn and fabric.[85]

TEXTILE PRODUCTION PROCESS IN THE COLONIES

By the late 17th century, all classes of people throughout the colonies were spinning and producing textiles, from the poor to the well-to-do. Smaller homes had some textile equipment and moderate access to fibers for textile production

Figure 2.14 Image of a small Rhode Island home constructed in 1700. (George J. Vaillancourt, Historic American Buildings Survey, *Fireplace House, Entrance "A" Road to Lincoln Woods Reservation, Saylesville, Providence County, RI*, 1933, photograph, Library of Congress.)

in the home, while larger plantations had plots of hemp and flax for linen production with onsite spinners and weavers.[86] In both instances, there was a need for similar textile equipment to turn homegrown fibers into colonial homespun cloth. Spinning was the first step in preparing a fiber for weaving. The task of spinning was often assigned to an unmarried sister or older daughter living at home. On large estates or plantations, the task of spinning fibers on a spinning wheel was given to female servants or slaves.[87]

The largest spinning wheel was called a 'walking wheel,' or 'great wheel,' and was used for spinning wool. The process required an older girl or woman to spin the larger wheel with her right hand as she walked backward alongside the wheel, while pulling and twisting fibers with her left hand from the tip of the wheel's spindle. The spinner then walked forward alongside the wheel to wrap the twisted yarn onto the base of the spindle. This process was repeated until the spindle was full of yarn.[88] In a small, lower-income home, spinning could be done with a simple device known as a drop spindle. The stick-like wooden tool relied on gravity to work. A wooden disk was attached to one end of the stick. On the other end of the stick, a spinner attached fibers from a bundle or a distaff. While the spinner held the fiber bundle or distaff with one hand, the other hand worked with the drop spindle to pull down and twist a continuous strand of yarn. Once the disk hit the ground with the length of the spun fiber, she wound the twisted yarn around the stick and began the spinning process again.[89]

After the spinning process was complete, the yarn was unwound from a spindle, measured for length, and rolled into skeins. The process of measuring and winding yarn could be done by hand or by using a wooden niddy-noddy or click reel.[90] Wound skeins of yarn were washed, sometimes dyed, and then placed on a yarn-winder. From the yarn-winder, yarn could be wound into balls for creating knit garments or woven cloth.[91] In order to prepare yarn for a weaver, wooden spools were wound for the warp of the cloth, while quills were wound for the weft. Quills were bobbins made to fit into a weaving shuttle that a weaver used to pass weft yarns back and forth through the warp yarns to create cloth.[92]

The most common loom construction used in the early colonies was referred to as a 'pair of looms.' The name came from the construction of two identical wooden frames that were joined at the end with cross bars. The width of the loom was based on the stretch of the weaver's arms as they threw the shuttle across the raised warp yarns with one hand, while catching it with the other. To create cloth, warp yarns were stretched out vertically in front of the weaver on the loom. In early

Figure 2.15 A walking wheel and loom located in the mid-17th century Fairbanks House of Dedham, Massachusetts. Jonathan Fairbanks, original owner of the home, was a spinning wheel maker. (Frank T. Deyette, Thomas T. Waterman, and Stanley Mixon, Historic American Buildings Survey, *Jonathan Fairbanks House, 511 East Street, Dedham, MA*, 1933, photograph, Library of Congress.)

loom construction, warp threads passed through at least two harnesses. The foot treadles, connected to the harness system of the loom, were pressed down creating a passage in the warp yarns for the shuttle to pass through horizontally. The newly thrown horizontal weft yarn was then driven into the cloth with a wooden bar called a beater. This process was repeated until the warp yarns attached to the loom were full of weft yarn. The completed cloth was then cut from the loom.[93]

In the early colonial home, spinning wheels greatly outnumbered looms in late 17th century New England. Most households sent their spun yarn out of the home to be woven by trained weavers in the community.[94] These community weavers were essential to the system of creating cloth in the colonies. At least 13 percent of the men who immigrated to the Massachusetts Bay Colony were trained in English weaving workshops before coming to the colonies.[95] Colonial male weavers were often farmers who oversaw the day-to-day management of their property, fields, and livestock, while weaving in between agricultural activities. An advantage of this system was the ability to grow their own hemp and flax as well as raise sheep for textile production.[96]

Other colonial weavers set up textile shops with apprentices and journeymen. Between the late 17th century and early 18th century, Connecticut weaver Christopher Leffingwell, with his apprentices and journeyman, produced 15 different types

Figure 2.16 A drop spindle. (*Spindle*, wood and iron, 13 7/16 x 3 3/16 in (34.2 x 8.1 cm), Rogers Fund 1914. Courtesy of The Metropolitan Museum of Art.)

of cloth.[97] The apprentice in a weaving shop was given the skills necessary to make a living when the apprenticeship was over. After an apprenticeship ended, the apprentice became a journeyman who found work with another master weaver. Journeymen often stayed with a master weaver until they could save up enough money to purchase all the tools and raw materials needed to set up their own weaving shop.[98] While boys could apprentice as weavers, girls in a weaver's home could learn skills from their father but never become a master weaver. A female who produced homemade cloth was called a 'cottage' or vernacular weaver.[99] While professionally trained male weavers produced fancy cloth, home-trained vernacular female weavers were known to produce the simpler, basic woven fabrics needed in every household.[100]

CHILDREN ASSIGNED TO TEXTILE AND CLOTHING PRODUCTION

In the 17th-century network of household and community cloth production, adults and children alike participated in the production of textiles. Spinning was a task that children were often given in the creation of textiles. In colonial homes, girls primarily spun fiber, but small boys were also taught the art of spinning.[101] In a weaver's home, his children could wind yarn onto the quill in preparation for weaving the weft yarn as well as wind the spools needed for the warp yarn.[102] In most homes, girls and boys were taught to knit by the age of six. These children were responsible for knitting all of the stockings and mittens for members of the household. Embroidery was another skill learned by these young knitters. After a pair of stockings was completed, the initials of the person wearing the items were stitched into the garments.[103]

Learning the skills of knitting, embroidery, and plain sewing enabled a girl in the household to construct simple garments. By the age of eight, a girl trained as an indentured servant could work as a seamstress in the home they were contracted to.[104] Children involved in textile production not only included those born to colonial parents, but poor children brought to America for labor as well as Indigenous and African children bound as servants or slaves. *New England's First Fruits*, published in 1643, describes the process of bringing poor children from England specifically to assist in textile manufacturing.[105]

CLOTHING

ANGLO-EUROPEAN UPPER-CLASS CHILDREN'S CLOTHING

Clothing for children of colonial times could be quite simple, elaborate, or nonexistent, depending

Figure 2.17 Illustration of an older woman using a drop spindle and a distaff to spin fibers. (Francisco de Goya y Lucientes, *An old woman spinning, spindle in her right hand, distaff in her left*, 1819, pen lithograph, 6 1/4 × 5 1/8 in (15.8 × 13 cm). Courtesy of The Metropolitan Museum of Art.)

on the social status of the child. In wealthier families, most of the fabrics purchased for clothing were imported, as was the case for the family of Maryland plantation owner Robert Cole. Upon his death in 1662, all seven of his children were clothed by a tailor who came yearly to make new clothes from imported fabrics and lace, as well as mend clothes worn the previous year. This yearly visit by the employed tailor lasted for a span of ten years for the Cole children.[106] The few existing portraits of wealthy children in colonial America, painted by the Freake-Gibbs painter, give us a glimpse of the clothing practices of high-status families in the late 17th century. The identity of the Freake-Gibbs painter is unknown, but what remains of the artist's work is a series of paintings commissioned by affluent parents to have their children captured on canvas. This series of paintings has become the only visual imagery we have of colonial American children in the late 17th century. The paintings of the Mason children, their younger sister Alice, and the Gibbs children, detail clothing for boys and girls between the ages of two and eight.[107]

The painting of Alice Mason was identified for several centuries as the portrait of a young John Quincy. This misidentification occurred due to the portrait passing down through the family of Abigail Adams and the fact that clothing for small boys and girls in the 17th century was very similar.[108] The portrait of Alice details a child under the age of three wearing similar clothing to her sisters in the painting of the Mason children. Alice Mason,

Figure 2.18 A mid-18th-century wooden click reel used for measuring and winding yarn. (*Click Reel*, wood, mid-18th century, photograph, Newbury, MA. From the collections of the Museum of Old Newbury.)

Figure 2.19 Dyed skeins of wool yarn. (Russel Lee, *Dyed woolen skeins of thread at WPA weaving project*, 1939, photograph, Library of Congress.)

Figure 2.20 A weaver's wooden shuttles with quills placed inside. Initials of the weaver are carved on the back. (*Weaver's shuttles with quills*, wood, 1760–1810, photograph, Newbury, MA. From the collections of the Museum of Old Newbury.)

Figure 2.21 Illustration of a Quaker master weaver in Pennsylvania weaving on a loom. (Julius Friedrich Sachse, *Ephrata, a woodcut showing a brother weaving cloth on an old hand loom*, 1890, woodcut reproduction, 11 x 13 cm (4 x 5 in), Library of Congress.)

Figure 2.22 Close-up view of a linen sample. The warp threads are vertical, and the weft threads are horizontal. (*Linen sample*, 4.5 x 4.5 in (11.3 x 11.3 cm). Photograph taken by the author.)

Figure 2.23 Illustrated plans for an early American farm. (Patrick Campbell, *Plan of an American New Cleared Farm*, 1793, engraving, 24.5 x 32.5 cm (9.6 x 12.7 in). Courtesy of the John Carter Brown Library.)

Figure 2.24 A young woman weaving on a traditional wooden loom at the Berry School. The Berry School was created by Martha Berry for the education of poor children in the rural South. (*The weaving room, Berry School, Mount Berry Ga.*, 1900, photograph, Library of Congress.)

age two, Abigail Mason, age six, and Joanna Mason, age four, are all wearing dark-colored gowns with a single slashed sleeve, finished with ribbon ties at the elbow. Under the dark gowns are fine linen shifts with puffed ruffled sleeves, which end below the sleeves of the gowns. Worn over the children's gowns are long, white-skirted aprons with V-shaped fitted bodices. The cap sleeves of the apron bodices as well as the rounded necks are edged in lace. As was customary in the 17th century, it is likely all three children were wearing padded stays underneath their gowns.

Regardless of social class among European or English children, after a young boy was breeched, he then followed the clothing practices of his father. In the case of the Mason children of Massachusetts, painted in 1670, the oldest child David is dressed in a style reminiscent of the petticoat breeches worn by fashionable men of Europe at the time. Like the adult fashion, eight-year-old David is wearing a puffed undershirt tucked into petticoat breeches. Petticoat breeches consisted of a full, divided skirt worn over a pair of loose linen drawers.

Petticoat breeches were paired with a short bolero-styled jacket with slashed open sleeves. David's ensemble is finished with an open front square fallen collar edged in lace.[109] In contrast to David's male attire is Margaret Gibbs' clothing at age seven, also painted by the Freake-Gibbs painter.

In Margaret's portrait, she is dressed in a style similar to women's clothing of the time, in contrast to Joanne and Abigail Mason. Under Margaret's bodice and skirt is a fine linen chemise with ruffled sleeves edged in lace. The sleeves are tied at the

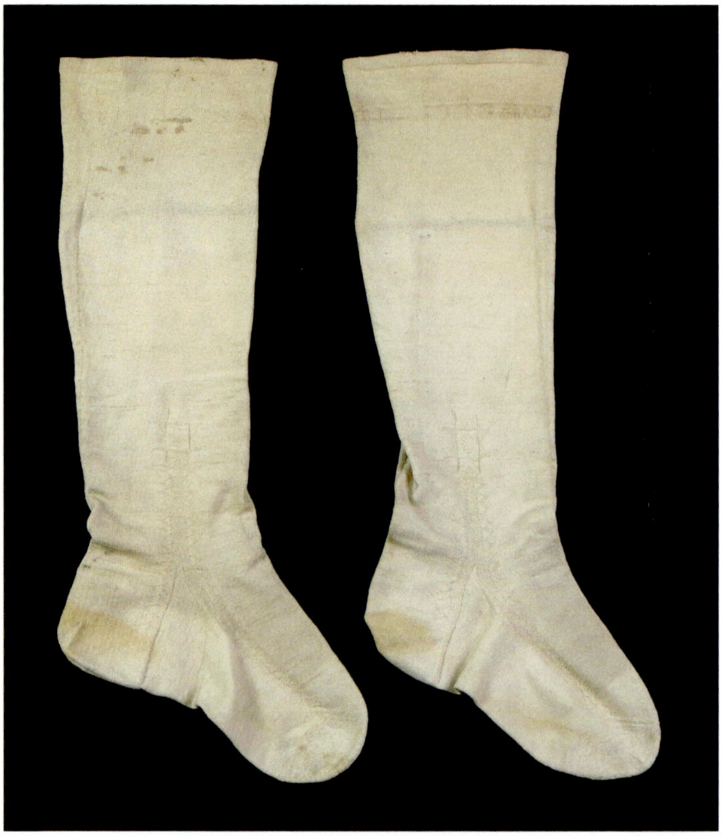

Figure 2.25 A pair of children's cotton-knit stockings from the early 19th century. (*Stockings*, cotton, 1807, gift of the Brooklyn Museum, 2009. Courtesy of The Metropolitan Museum of Art.)

Figure 2.26 Illustration of John Quincy now identified as Alice Mason. (*John Quincy, 1689–1767*, 1929, The Miriam and Ira D. Wallach Division of Art, Prints and Photographs: Print Collection. Courtesy of The New York Public Library.)

Figure 2.27 Portrait of David, Joanna, and Abigail Mason. (Freake-Gibbs Painter, *David, Joanna, and Abigail Mason*, 1670, painting, 1003.3 x 1079.5 in (2548.3 x 2741.9 cm), gift of Mr. and Mrs. John D Rockefeller 3rd. Courtesy of the DeYoung Museum.)

Figure 2.28 Portrait of Margaret Gibbs. (Freake-Gibbs painter, *Margaret Gibbs*, 1670, oil on canvas, 102.87 x 84.14 cm (40 1/2 x 33 1/8 in), bequest of Elsie Q. Giltinan. Courtesy of the Museum of Fine Arts, Boston.)

elbow with a colorful ribbon placed in between the puff of the sleeve and the bottom ruffle. The flat bodice seems to have a soft curve at the bottom edge with slashed, short, puffed sleeves finished at the edge with a band of fabric. Also attached to the back of the bodice are hanging sleeves which have been pinned up to keep the sleeves from dragging behind Margaret. Worn over the bodice and skirt is a bibbed apron that may have been constructed in two pieces. The cut of the apron bib is wide at the neck, extending into the armscye, and then narrows as it meets the bottom edge of the bodice. The gathered skirt of the apron appears to be tucked under the bodice and apron bib. Both the apron bib and skirt are finished off with a delicate patterned trim. Margaret also wears a sheer linen collar trimmed in a wide needle lace. The collar has been constructed to lie flat as it curves around Margaret's shoulders and the short sleeves of the bodice.

NEW ENGLAND CLOTHING REGULATIONS

In the case of David and Margaret, their clothes not only reflected the dress of their parents, but also mirrored the sumptuary laws of the Massachusetts Bay Colony. Early in colonial New England, Puritan ministers used their influence on the General Court system to enact laws prohibiting excess in clothing. At a time in fashion history when a series of slashes on an outer garment revealed the color of an underlayer, New England colonists could only have one slash on each sleeve and one slash in the back of a garment. The use of gold, silver, or lace in everyday clothing was also forbidden. In the mid-17th century, further sumptuary laws prohibited colonists of lower economic means to dress above their class. Only prosperous colonists, who possessed an estate valued at 200 pounds or more, could wear expensive fabrics and clothing. Officials of every town in the colony monitored dress and issued criminal indictments for anyone who broke a sumptuary law.[110]

In addition to sumptuary laws used to delineate class, colors also played a part in social status. Black was reserved for the 'best clothes' of leaders and elders in the community. The general population dressed in what was referred to as 'sadd' colors.[111] Everyday clothes were dyed using a variety of vegetables, plants, trees, and soot. The shades of colors produced by these natural ingredients included orange-browns or russet tones, soft reds, blues, greens, yellows, browns, grays, and purples.[112] Seventeenth-century inventories contain colors used to describe cloth or clothing pieces, such as liver color, dead leaf, tawney, French green, flax blossom, puce, russet, violet, and ginger lyne. In contrast to these 'sadd' colors, women and children often wore brightly colored ribbons to offset the subdued shades of their clothing.[113] Looking again at the portraits of Alice Mason, the Mason children, and Margaret Gibbs, the Freake-Gibbs artist not only captured the sumptuary laws of the time, but the prominent New England color palette as well.

ANGLO-EUROPEAN MIDDLE CLASS AND POOR CHILDREN'S CLOTHING

In contrast to Upper-class children, children of more humble means were dressed in homemade garments primarily made from homespun fabrics. The more common household wardrobe was simple, with few garments per family member. Repairing, reusing, and remodeling clothing was an economical way to save time and money in the colonial home. When the time came to create new clothing, women in these households could use worn-through garments as patterns for cutting new garments and enlist the aid of their children in the construction. Due to the time-intensive work of making new clothing for family members, wardrobes were kept small in an industrious home. Women and their daughters might have one or two under shifts, a pair of stays, several petticoats, a waistcoat, an apron, one or two caps, and stockings. The male members of the household, over the age of six, might have simple breeches, often made of leather, a few shirts, a jacket, and stockings.[114]

Poor children had even less clothing and moved into adult clothing much faster than children of higher status. In the instance of poor children bound to service, clothing was provided by their master in most contracts. In the terms of an apprentice contract, a male child would receive food, lodging, clothing, and an education in the art of the master's trade.[115] At the end of an apprenticeship, the legal minimum of freedom dues for a master to provide was one to two suits of clothing. One suit was equal to five months of wages for a laborer. If a master was invested in the success of his apprentice, in addition to suits of clothing, the young man could receive a sum of money, land, or tools of the trade at the end of his apprenticeship.[116]

INDIGENOUS AND AFRICAN CHILDREN'S CLOTHING IN COLONIAL HOMES

Indigenous children, who were placed in colonial homes as servants or slaves were quickly placed in simple European or English-style clothing provided by their master. Dress for Indigenous servants was similar to the European and English garments worn

Figure 2.29 Child's small undyed short-sleeved linen dress with a simple block print pattern of flowers, leaves, and berries in red madder. The sleeves are made from several small pieces of linen carefully stitched together. (*Child's dress,* 1780–1790, linen, gift of the New England Historical Genealogical Society. Courtesy of Historic New England.)

Figure 2.30 View of a pieced sleeve from the child's small, undyed, short-sleeved linen dress. (*Child's dress*, 1780–1790, gift of the New England Historical Genealogical Society. Courtesy of Historic New England.)

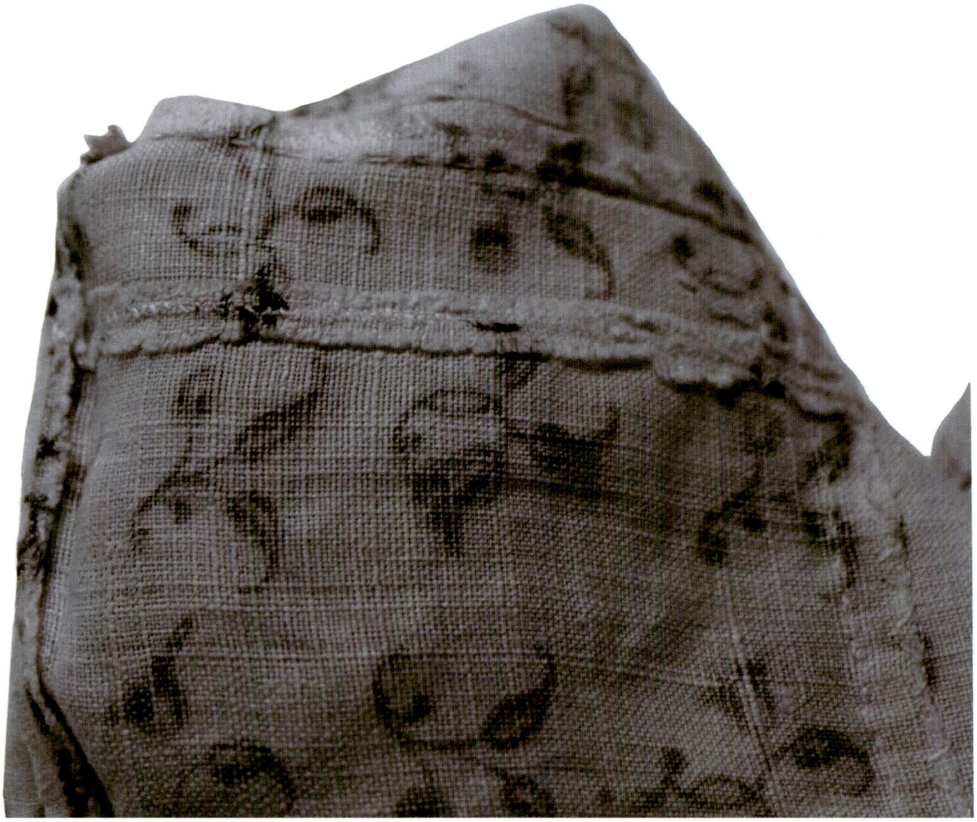

Figure 2.31 Construction view of a pieced sleeve from the child's small, undyed, short-sleeved linen dress. (*Child's dress*, 1780–1790, gift of the New England Historical Genealogical Society. Courtesy of Historic New England.)

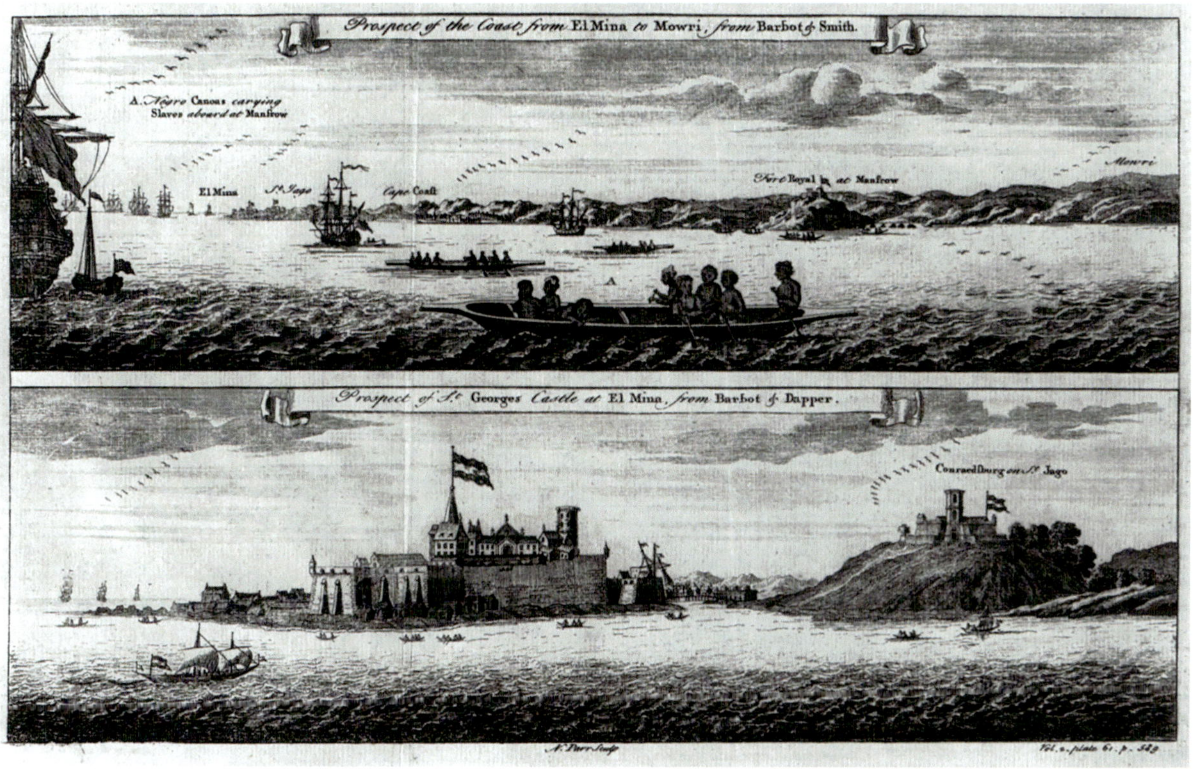

Figure 2.32 Illustration of African captives off the Gold Coast of Africa in small boats as they are taken to large slave ships in the harbor. (*2 views of the Gold Coast of Africa. "Prospect of the Coast from Elmina to Mowri," showing slaves being loaded on ship in foreground; "Prospect of St. Georges Castle at Elimina,"* 1745, copper engraving, Library of Congress.)

by 'praying town' residents. Advertisements for runaway Indigenous servants describe male servants wearing breeches, trousers, jackets, shirts, coats, and waistcoats. Female servants were described as wearing simple gowns, or short gowns, with petticoats, aprons, and shifts.[117] In contrast to Indigenous children, African enslaved children were clothed in very little or nothing at all. A firsthand account given by Augustino, a West African survivor of a harrowing journey through the middle passage as an enslaved 12-year-old boy, revealed that captured men, women, and children were stripped of their clothing once they boarded slave ships off the coast of Africa. The captain of the ship was solely in charge of whether his human cargo received cloth to cover themselves. While some captains did provide cloth for their naked captives, others did not.[118]

The practice of choosing to clothe enslaved African children or not was also witnessed on Barbados plantations, which carried over to the early American plantation system. If a plantation master was profit-minded, the children on his plantation were not clothed in order to save money and the labor it took to create the clothing.[119] Small children, who were not given garments, were wrapped in cloth remnants during the winter months or given worn clothing items handed down from enslaved family members. In these cases, simple clothing, similar to the dress of enslaved adults, was made for enslaved children once they reached puberty. Male slaves primarily wore a pair of trousers, a shirt, and a jacket often with no shoes or stockings.[120] If a master did provide clothing for his enslaved children, male children were given a simple shirt to wear, while

Figure 2.33 Illustration of an African enslaved mother and father with two small children. The children are not clothed. The mother is holding a drop spindle with fibers wound on the spindle. (John Gabriel Stedman, Famiglia di Schiayi Negri di Loango, 1818, etching, 10.7 x 6.3 cm (4.2 x 2.4 in). Courtesy of the John Carter Brown Library.)

female children wore a simple shift dress. The wives of plantation owners were often responsible for making all of the clothing items for enslaved men, women, and children, with the help of enslaved young girls and women on the plantation. Regarding footwear, no shoes were given to enslaved children until the cold months of the year.[121]

As the 17th century ended, early American colonial officials saw to it that poor, orphaned, Indigenous, African, and mixed-race children became a substantial part of the laboring workforce. Due to the Navigation Acts, colonists had no choice but to create systems in the home and in the community for focused textile production. Incorporating children in the tasks of spinning fibers and constructing garments in the newly formed Anglo-European colonies made textile and clothing production possible. Regarding clothing, children from wealthy families were dressed in more intricately designed and constructed garments, while children of lower means wore simple clothing items. In the case of servants and enslaved children, their clothing could range from simple pieces similar to that of servants and enslaved adults, or they were not given garments to wear until puberty. The decision of what children wore was most often made by a parent, a guardian, or a master.

NOTES

1 Susan M. Ouellette, *US Textile Production in Historical Perspective: A Case Study from Massachusetts* (New York: Routledge; Taylor and Francis Group, 2012), 47, 49.

2 Alan Gallay, *The Indian Slave Trade: The Rise of the English Empire in the American South, 1670–1717* (New Haven: Yale University Press, 2002), 57; Peter H. Wood, *Black Majority* (New York: W. W. Norton & Company, 1974), 39; Denise I. Bossy, "Godin & Co.: Charleston Merchants and the Indian Trade, 1674–1715," *The South Carolina Historical Magazine* 114, no. 2 (2013): 97.

3 Andrés Reséndez, *The Other Slavery* (Boston: Mariner Books, 2016), 50.

4 Gallay, *The Indian Slave Trade*, 57; Wood, *Black Majority*, 39; Bossy, "Godin & Co.: Charleston Merchants," 97.

5 Peter Kolchin, *American Slavery 1619–1877* (New York: Hill and Wang, 2003), 7–9, 12.

6 Kathleen A. Staples and Madelyn Shaw, *Clothing Through American History* (Oxford: Greenwood, 2013), 83.

7 Staples and Shaw, *Clothing Through American History*, 9.

8 Jenny Hale Pulsipher, *Subjects unto the Same King: Indians, English, and the Context for Authority in Colonial New England* (Philadelphia: University of Pennsylvania Press, 2005), 72.

9 Edmund S. Morgan, *The Puritan Family: Religion and Domestic Relations in Seventeenth-Century New England* (Mansfield Centre: Martino Publishing, 2014), 37–38.

10 Ruth Wallis Herndon and John E. Murray, eds., *Children Bound to Labor: The Pauper Apprentice System in Early America* (Ithaca: Cornell University Press, 2009), 4.

11 Ouellette, *US Textile Production in Historical Perspective*, 47, 49; Morgan, *The Puritan Family*, 28.

12 David Hackett Fischer, *Albion's Seed: Four British Folkways in America* (New York: Oxford University Press, 1989), 101.
13 Alysa Levene, "Parish Apprenticeship and the Old Poor Law in London," *The Economic History Review* 63, no. 4 (2010): 916–18, www.jstor.org/stable/40929865; Herndon and Murray, *Children Bound to Labor*, 1, 2.
14 Herndon and Murray, 8, 15, 37; John E. Murray and Ruth Wallis Herndon, "Markets for Children in Early America: A Political Economy of Pauper Apprenticeship," *The Journal of Economic History* 62, no. 2 (2002): 359, www.jstor.org/stable/2698184.
15 Levene, "Parish Apprenticeship," 916–18.
16 Barry Levy, "Girls and Boys: Poor Children and the Labor Market in Colonial Massachusetts," *Pennsylvania History: A Journal of Mid-Atlantic Studies* 64 (1997): 290–93, www.jstor.org/stable/27774064.
17 Murray and Herndon, "Markets for Children in Early America," 365–67.
18 Herndon and Murray, 1–2.
19 Winthrop D. Jordan, "The Influence of the West Indies on the Origins of New England Slavery," *The William and Mary Quarterly* 18, no. 2 (1961): 245–47, https://doi.org/10.2307/1918546.
20 Kathleen J. Bragdon, *Native People of Southern New England: 1500 to 1650* (Norman: University of Oklahoma Press, 1996), 213.
21 Ann Marie Plane, *Colonial Intimacies: Indian Marriage in Early New England* (Ithaca: Cornell University Press, 2000), 102.
22 Richard Middleton and Anne Lombard, *Colonial America: A History to 1763*, 4th ed. (West Sussex: Wiley-Blackwell, 2011), 172.
23 Plane, *Colonial Intimacies*, 101.
24 Bragdon, *Native People: 1500–1650*, 212.
25 Morgan, 63.
26 Jared Ross Hardesty, *Black Lives, Native Lands, White Worlds: A History of Slavery in New England* (Boston, MA: Bright Leaf, 2019), 28.
27 Ronald Bailey, "The Slave(ry) Trade and the Development of Capitalism in the United States: The Textile Industry in New England," *Social Science History* 14, no. 3 (1990): 379–80, https://doi.org/10.2307/1171357.
28 Ronald Bailey, "The Other Side of Slavery: Black Labor, Cotton, and Textile Industrialization in Great Britain and the United States," *Agricultural History* 68, no. 2 (1994): 45, 47, www.jstor.org/stable/3744401.
29 Bailey, "The Slave(ry) Trade and the Development of Capitalism," 382–83, 378.
30 Gloria McCahon Whiting, "Race, Slavery, and the Problem of Numbers in Early New England: A View from Probate Court," *The William and Mary Quarterly* 77, no. 3 (2020): 418–21, 426.
31 Carter G. Woodson, "The Negro in New England," *Negro History Bulletin* 5, no. 1 (1941): 5, www.jstor.org/stable/44246616.
32 Dominik Nagl, "The Governmentality of Slavery in Colonial Boston, 1690–1760," *Amerikastudien/American Studies* 58, no. 1 (2013): 8, www.jstor.org/stable/43485857.
33 Woodson, "The Negro in New England," 5–6.
34 Warren M. Billings and David Hackett Fischer, "Sir William Berkeley – Portrait by Fischer: A Critique," *The William and Mary Quarterly* 48, no. 4 (1991): 600, https://doi.org/10.2307/2938123.
35 Fischer, *Albion's Seed*, 212–14.
36 Fischer, 243; Gallay, 31.
37 Kolchin, *American Slavery*, 12.
38 Middleton and Lombard, *Colonial America*, 121.
39 Lois Green Carr and Lorena S. Walsh, "The Planter's Wife: The Experience of White Women in Seventeenth Century Maryland," *The William and Mary Quarterly* 34, no. 4 (1977): 542–43, https://doi.org/10.2307/2936182.
40 Herndon and Murray, 184.
41 Howard Mackey, "The Operation of the English Old Poor Law in Colonial Virginia," *The Virginia Magazine of History and Biography* 73, no. 1 (1965): 34, www.jstor.org/stable/4247080.
42 Murray and Herndon, 357.
43 Herndon and Murray, 185.
44 Herndon and Murray, 184.
45 Abbot Emerson Smith, "The Indentured Servant and Land Speculation in Seventeenth Century Maryland," *The American Historical Review* 40, no. 3 (1935): 468–70, https://doi.org/10.2307/1838904; Richard J. Purcell, "Irish Colonists in Colonial Maryland," *Studies: An Irish Quarterly Review* 23, no. 90 (1934): 279, www.jstor.org/stable/30095145.
46 Middleton and Lombard, 127.
47 Herndon and Murray, 5, 52.
48 A. J. Morrison, "The Virginia Indian Trade to 1673," *The William and Mary Quarterly* 1, no. 4 (1921): 226, https://doi.org/10.2307/1915333.

49 Robbie Ethridge and Sheri M. Shuck-Hall, eds., *Mapping the Mississippian Shatter Zone: The Colonial Indian Slave Trade and Regional Insta* (University of Nebraska Press, 2009), 295–98, https://doi.org/10.2307/j.ctt1dgn4d8.

50 James D. Rice, "Bacon's Rebellion in Indian Country," *The Journal of American History* 101, no. 3 (2014): 744–45, www.jstor.org/stable/44286295.

51 Jonathan L. Alpert, "The Origin of Slavery in the United States-The Maryland Precedent," *The American Journal of Legal History* 14, no. 3 (1970): 190, 192, 197, https://doi.org/10.2307/844413.

52 Fischer, 11.

53 Fischer, 12.

54 William A. Pettigrew, "Free to Enslave: Politics and the Escalation of Britain's Transatlantic Slave Trade, 1688–1714," *The William and Mary Quarterly* 64, no. 1 (2007): 5, www.jstor.org/stable/4491595.

55 Margaret Ellen Newell, *Brethren by Nature: New England Indians, Colonists, and the Origins of American Slavery* (Ithaca: Cornell University Press, 2015), 104–7.

56 A. B. Wilkinson, *Blurring the Lines of Race & Freedom: Mulattoes & Mixed Bloods in English Colonial America* (Chapel Hill: University of Nort Carolina Press, 2020), 27, 36, 45–48.

57 Wilkinson, *Blurring the Lines*, 64.

58 "The Colleton Family in South Carolina," *The South Carolina Historical and Genealogical Magazine* 1, no. 4 (1900): 325–27, www.jstor.org/stable/27574930.

59 Middleton and Lombard, 149–55.

60 Daragh Grant, "'Civilizing' the Colonial Subject: The Co-Evolution of State and Slavery in South Carolina, 1670–1739," *Comparative Studies in Society and History* 57, no. 3 (2015): 613, www.jstor.org/stable/43908365; Thomas J. Little, "The South Carolina Slave Laws Reconsidered, 1670–1700," *The South Carolina Historical Magazine* 94, no. 2 (1993): 87, www.jstor.org/stable/27569914.

61 Wood, 16.

62 Gallay, 16.

63 Gallay, 16.

64 Gallay, 4.

65 Bossy, 111–12.

66 Gallay, 57; Wood, 39; Bossy, 97.

67 Gallay, 60–63.

68 Staples and Shaw, 10.

69 Reséndez, *The Other Slavery*, 50.

70 Wood, 36.

71 Little, "South Carolina Slave Laws Reconsidered," 90, 100, 101.

72 Grant, "'Civilizing' the Colonial Subject," 615.

73 Ouellette, 6, 10.

74 Middleton and Lombard, 139.

75 Middleton and Lombard, 139.

76 Ouellette, 10, 32.

77 Laurel Thatcher Ulrich, *The Age of Homespun: Objects and Stories in the Creation of an American Myth* (New York: Vintage Books, 2001), 51.

78 Ouellette, 30–31.

79 George B. Blodgette, *Early Settlers of Rowley, Massachusetts: A Genealogical Record of the Families Who Settled in Rowley before 1700, with Several Generations of Their Descendants* (Rowley, MA: Essex Institute Historical Collections, 1933), 272, 273, Internet Archive.

80 Ouellette, 78.

81 Staples and Shaw, 151.

82 Staples and Shaw, 152.

83 Thomas J. Wertenbaker, *The Planters of Colonial Virginia* (Princeton: Princeton University Press, 1922), 92, 103.

84 Victor S. Clark, *History of Manufactures in the United States 1607–1860* (Washington, DC: Carnegie Institute of Washington, 1916), 32–39.

85 William R. Bagnall, *The Textile Industries of the United States*, vol. 1 (Cambridge: Riverside Press, 1893), 8–9, Google Books; Middleton and Lombard, 177.

86 Wertenbaker, *The Planters of Colonial Virginia*, 108.

87 Susan Burrows Swan, *Plain & Fancy: American Women and Their Needlework, 1700–1850* (New York: Routledge, 1977), 22.

88 Swan, *Plain & Fancy*, 20.

89 Ulrich, *The Age of Homespun*, 87.

90 Peter M. Molloy, *Homespun to Factory Made: Woolen Textiles in America, 1776–1876* (North Andover: Merrimack Valley Textile Museum, 1976), 22.

91 Ulrich, 92.

92 Staples and Shaw, 86.

93 Ulrich, 92; Molloy, *Homespun to Factory*, 36; Staples and Shaw, 87.

94 Staples and Shaw, 144.

95 Ouellette, 45, 53.

96 Ulrich, 86.

97 Ouellette, 86.

98 Herndon and Murray, 204.

99 Ouellette, 87, 89.

100 Ouellette, 87, 89.
101 Staples and Shaw, 83.
102 Molloy, 24.
103 Swan, 24–25.
104 Swan, 24–25.
105 *New England's First Fruits: With Divers other Special Matters Concerning that Country* (London: R. O. and G. D. for Henry Overton, 1643), 42.
106 Staples and Shaw, 111.
107 Henry Adams, "Freake Out!" *The Magazine Antiques*, September 3, 2021, www.themagazineantiques.com/article/freake-out/.
108 Adams, "Freake Out!".
109 Estelle Ansley Worrell, *Children's Costume in America 1607–1910* (New York: Charles Scribner's Sons, 1980), 18.
110 George Francis Dow, *Every Day Life in the Massachusetts Bay Colony* (New York: Dover Publications, 1988), 62–63.
111 John Demos, *A Little Commonwealth: Family Life in Plymouth Colony*, 2nd ed. (Oxford: Oxford University Press, 2000), 53–54.
112 Demos, *A Little Commonwealth*, 53–54.
113 Fischer, 140.
114 Swan, 22.
115 Morgan, 72.
116 Murray and Herndon, 362.
117 Staples and Shaw, 51; Gallay, 303.
118 Wilma King, *African American Children: Historical Perspectives from Slavery to Civil Rights* (New York: Palgrave Macmillan, 2005), 12.
119 Jordan, "The Influence of the West Indies," 249.
120 Staples and Shaw, 51.
121 Wilma King, *Stolen Children: Slave Youth in Nineteenth Century America* (Bloomington: Indiana University Press, 1995), 15.

CHAPTER THREE

1700–1758

Leading up to 1700, England experienced several shifts in rulers. With the death of Charles II, came the monarchy of his Catholic brother, James II. James II was determined that England should become a Catholic kingdom once more during his short reign. Tensions between Protestant and Catholic citizens in England and the North American colonies escalated to the Glorious Revolution of 1689, which displaced James II as monarch. The new rulers of England supported by Parliament, were Mary, his Protestant daughter, and her husband William of Orange. This change in leadership was felt by the 250,000 inhabitants of the colonies, even though their geographical location was somewhat removed from England. With the death of Mary and William, Mary's younger sister ascended the throne in 1702. Though often overlooked by history, Queen Anne proved to be a successful monarch.[1] At the time of her passing, in 1714, the new Georgian era dawned with the coronation of George I. As political turmoil in England ebbed and flowed, colonial expansion was moving forward with continued immigration to North America and the establishment of all 13 colonies by 1732.[2]

With the founding of all 13 colonies, the plantation economy of the southern colonies drove the need for more labor, both Indigenous and African. In an effort to bind more Indigenous and African people into a lifetime of labor, laws began to categorize anyone of mixed Indigenous, African, or European ancestry as a slave.[3] Enslaved children became a large investment for plantation owners when laws passed in the 1740s deemed slaves as chattels of their masters.[4] Textiles played a large role in purchasing more African slaves in the early 18th century with the expansion of the plantation system.[5] A greater need to produce more textiles for growing colonial communities and plantations led to solidifying the use of child labor in the creation of cloth.[6] Large-scale textile production was seen in New England, New York, Pennsylvania, Maryland, and Virginia. With this expansion of textile production, colonists could choose from an assortment of local fabrics as well as a variety of ways cloth could be dyed or printed.[7] Clothing for poor or enslaved children in the early 18th century was most often limited, very simple in construction, and made of coarse, unfinished cloth. In contrast, children of the middle to upper social classes possessed many more clothing items made from a collection of finer finished fabrics.

DOI: 10.4324/9781003230441-4

COMMUNITIES: SOCIAL AND POLITICAL STRUCTURE

SOUTHERN COMMUNITIES

Indigenous Slavery

Before the beginning of the 18th century, South Carolina had become the foremost Indigenous slave trader of North America.[8] The two groups of South Carolina colonists most involved with the Indigenous slave trade were plantation owners and Charles Town merchants.[9] Plantation owners used their involvement in the slave trade to finance their estates by purchasing labor and needed supplies, while raising their status in the colony. Charles Town merchants gained positions of power in the South Carolina economy as well as considerable wealth. These colonial slave traders often incited war between Native tribes to profit from the sale of noncombatant captives taken during tribal wars.[10] Indigenous wars provided Native captives to ensure the Indigenous slave trade remained profitable.[11] According to historical documentation, Indigenous slavery existed in all early English colonies.[12]

Captive Indigenous men, women, and children were transported to Charles Town where they were exported and sold to Boston, Rhode Island, Pennsylvania, New York, and Virginia as slaves.[13] The selling of Indigenous children began under the influence of English traders. A documented slave raid in 1707, orchestrated by English slave traders and Indigenous Savannah slave hunters, primarily enslaved children in the attack. A census taken a year later in South Carolina revealed that 41 percent of the white population, 29 percent of the Black population, and 15 percent of the Indigenous population were children.[14] The low number of Indigenous children in South Carolina points to the selling of these children to other colonies for labor.[15] South Carolina did keep a number of Indigenous child captives for labor. Between 1703 and 1708, more Indigenous slaves were recorded in South Carolina than African slaves.[16]

Figure 3.1 Illustration of Indigenous men, women, and children fleeing a burning village. (Alain René La Sage, 1732, engraving, 12.3 x 6.8 cm (4.8 x 2.6 in). Courtesy of the John Carter Brown Library.)

As the Carolina slave trade expanded in the early 18th century, Indigenous slave raids reached deep into Spanish Florida, specifically targeting the Indigenous people of Spanish missions.[17] Raids involving the South Carolina government, the Yamasee, and the Apalachicola crossed over into

Spanish Florida, devastating the Indigenous populations residing in the region. After 1711, there were no large Indigenous populations left to enslave in Florida due to a series of large-scale slave-hunting raids.[18] War, disease, and the estimated 20,000 Indigenous men, women, and children sold as slaves from Florida alone led to the severe decline of trading Native people for profit. Indigenous slave trading continued on a smaller scale, but wars used specifically to fuel the South Carolina slave trade came to an end.[19] As Indigenous slavery declined in the region, African slave labor rapidly increased.[20]

South Carolina was not the only southern colony involved in Indigenous slavery. Both North Carolina and Virginia preferred to sell their Indigenous captives to the West Indies.[21] Lower-class Virginia planters, particularly in the southwestern region, who could not afford to purchase imported African slaves, relied on regional Indigenous slave labor.[22] Due to the slave raids of the Westo and the Yamasee, in alliance with English and Scottish traders, the coastline of Georgia was depopulated of Indigenous men, women, and children years before the land was claimed as a colony by the English Crown in 1732.[23] Although the numbers of Indigenous men, women, and child slaves laboring in Georgia were much lower than South Carolina, Native slaves served the new colony at its beginning. Many of the Indigenous slaves brought to Georgia came with settlers who relocated to the new colony.[24]

Figure 3.2 Illustration of a Timucua Indigenous village located in North Central Florida. (Pieter van der Aa, *Native American Settlement*, 1707, engraving, 13.6 x 17.9 cm (5.3 x 7 in). Courtesy of the John Carter Brown Library.)

Figure 3.3 Illustration of a wedding celebration in a Timucua Indigenous village. (Pieter van der Aa, *Native American carry a woman on a litter*, 1707, engraving, 13.6 x 17.9 cm (5.3 x 7 in). Courtesy of the John Carter Brown Library.)

Scots-Irish Immigration

In the early 18th century, another large immigration influenced colonial expansion and displaced more Indigenous farmers and towns.[25] The political union of Scotland and England in 1707 allowed Scots equal access to opportunities available to those living under English rule.[26] An estimated 5,000 immigrants from Ireland, Scotland, and Northern England entered the colonies each year beginning in 1718 until the Revolutionary War. At least 150,000 immigrants came from Northern Ireland, often called the Ulster Scots.[27] Many of the Irish male immigrants were weavers by trade, escaping economic ruin due to the collapse of the wool and linen industries.[28] In South Carolina, they could receive a land grant of 200 acres each, which enabled them to establish farms with their families while continuing their work as weavers.[29]

African Slavery

While skilled Scots-Irish weavers chose to settle in the colonies to continue their craft of creating textiles for the surrounding community, others used textiles as a means to secure African slave captives from the transatlantic slave trade. Since the 1600s, when the East India Company was founded, textiles from India became the most valued commodity used to purchase slaves from Africa.[30] Large quantities of beautifully designed Indian cotton fabrics paid for African men, women, and children, who were transported and sold to plantation owners in colonial America. Colonial plantations then used

Figure 3.4 (Historic Buildings Survey, *Borough House Weaving Room, State Route 261 & Garners Ferry Road, Stateburg, Sumter County, SC*, 1933, photograph, Library of Congress.)

the purchased slaves to produce agricultural commodities for European buyers.[31] Scotsman Richard Oswald, co-owner of the Royal African Company in the 18th century, participated in this method of trade.[32]

Ships carrying manufactured goods left England to sail to India's textile manufacturing centers. From India, the ships traveled to West Africa's slave trading centers. Inexpensive Indian Madras textiles and human slaves were purchased on these journeys and then sold to plantation communities in the Caribbean and the southern colonies.[33] African slaves became less expensive and more accessible to Carolina planters due to the expanding English and colonial connections to the African slave trade.[34] To fulfill the growing need for labor on southern plantations, British traders were importing thousands of slaves from the Congo-Angola and Sierra Leone regions of West Africa. Sullivan Island, located in the Charles Town Harbor, became the key checkpoint for these enslaved African men, women, and children.[35] It is estimated over 40 percent of the African slave population between the years 1700 and 1775 was processed through Charles Town, South Carolina.[36] South Carolina quickly turned to African slavery, while they also continued their involvement in Indigenous enslavement.[37]

Beginning in 1720, an interesting turn of events occurred in South Carolina connected to slave classification. Interim Governor James Moore Jr. ordered a slave count in every parish of South Carolina resulting in the documentation of 6,525 colonists and 11,828 Black slaves.[38] Examination of the 1720 census reveals that those counted as Black slaves included any individual deemed a mixture of Indigenous, African, or European ancestry. While

Figure 3.5 A hand-painted palampore created in Madras (Chennai) India in the early 18th century. (*Palampore*, early 18th century, cotton, 84 x 114 ¼ in (213.4 x 290.2 cm), Rogers Fund 1915. Courtesy of the Metropolitan Museum of Art.)

the legislative body of South Carolina acknowledged the continuation of Indigenous slavery, they also declared mustees, mulattoes, and every slave not entirely Indigenous counted as a Negro and therefore was a slave for life.[39] To the colonial population in the 18th century, the term 'mulatto' categorized any individual who possessed a mixture of European, African, and Indigenous heritage. The term 'mustee' referred to an individual with a mixed heritage of Indigenous and African parentage.[40] Due to South Carolina's heavy involvement in both Indigenous and African slavery, the number of mustee children sentenced to a life of slavery was the largest of any southern colony.[41]

To further solidify slavery, in 1725, the acting governor of South Carolina, Arthur Middleton, referred to enslaved men, women, and children as goods and the chattels of their masters. This classification was legalized in 1740 as the slave population rose to 39,155.[42] In addition to the rising slave population in the region, slave shipments were coming directly from Africa. The ideal cargo for Carolina slaveholders consisted of boys and girls between the ages of 15 and 16. Plantation owners preferred boys, but girls were also bought at a ratio of two-thirds boys and one-third girls. Fifteen percent of the captured slaves coming from Africa were children under the age of ten.[43] By the middle of the 18th century, the slave population had reached 60,000. A southern planter aristocracy was now firmly established which depended on young African slaves.[44]

As with South Carolina, the first half of the 18th century saw African slavery become an integral part of Virginia and its plantation economy.[45] The idea that captured men, women, and children were already slaves when they were sold to Virginia planters made it easier to imbed slavery into the colony.[46] In 1705, Virginia lawmakers declared 'Negro,' 'Mulatto,' and 'Indian' slaves were similar to real estate and could pass down to heirs, similar to the custom of land inheritance.[47] This new legal classification was reflected in the estimated population rise of enslaved men, women, and children. In addition to the legalized classification of enslaved individuals, the end of the Royal African Company's monopoly on the slave trade led to a sharp increase in imported African labor to Virginia. Between the years 1700 and 1725, an estimated 27,800 African slaves were delivered directly to Virginia.[48] The slave population reached over 120,000 by 1756, while the estimated population of Virginia colonists was 173,000.[49] Wealthy Virginia planters viewed African slaves in particular as a source of imported revenue to be purchased for profitable gain.

A Virginia slave owner could choose to keep a slave family together in his possession or to sell them individually. A profit could be made from

Figure 3.6 Illustration of Charles Town Harbor in the mid-18th century. (Thomas Mellish, *A View of Charles Town the Capital of South Carolina*, 1768, engraving, 32.7 x 51 cm (12.8 x 20 in). Courtesy of the John Carter Brown Library.)

Figure 3.7 (*The African Slave Trade-Slaves Taken From a Dhow Captured by H.M.S. 'Undine,'* 1884, print from a wood engraving, *The Graphic*, June 1884, Library of Congress.)

selling the parents and the children individually if a master or mistress saw fit to do so.[50] In most instances, profit-focused planters in Virginia saw second-generation slave children as a gain from their initial investment. By purchasing first-generation African slaves who then had children, a planter's return doubled. The second-generation children immediately became the master's property and could be put to work in the plantation fields as soon as they were of age.[51] As time went on, slave children became a special commodity. Initially, slave traders tended to prefer men over women and children, however, in the first half of the 18th century, some slavers specifically dealt in selling children. While children over the age of ten were preferred as slaves, younger children were still sold into slavery.[52]

After being taken from their villages and transported to the African sea coast, children and adults were imprisoned while waiting for final processing. They were first stripped of their clothing, which enabled traders to thoroughly examine each captive in order to separate the able-bodied from the weak. The able-bodied were then branded with the name or symbol of the trading company they belonged to. Very little space was allotted for children on trading company slave ships as they traveled the middle passage; often, they were kept with the cargo on the lower deck of the ship after they were separated from adult family members.[53] This separation of children from their family would continue throughout the journey. Similar to adults on board slave ships, children were exposed to disease, starvation, physical abuse, and death on their

Figure 3.8 Detailed wooden model of a slave ship. (*Folk Art Model of a Slave Ship*, 1890–1950, wood and ivory, 6 1/8 × 21 × 6 in (15.6 × 53.3 × 15.2 cm). Collection of the Smithsonian National Museum of African American History and Culture.)

journey through the middle passage. If members of a family survived transportation, it was likely they were sold to different masters once they reached the colonial harbor, never to see each other again.[54]

NEW ENGLAND COMMUNITIES

Indigenous and African Slavery

The lives of the Indigenous population in New England were tenuous, at best.[55] While at war with the French northern territory during King William's War and Queen Ann's War in the late 17th and early 18th centuries, Indigenous women and children captives were taken and sold by Massachusetts troops. Indigenous males above the age of 12 were killed, while Indigenous women and children below the age of 12 were captured and sold as slaves. This pattern continued until 1760. At times, Indigenous captives were taken by army officers and used as workers in their homes.[56] The largest population of Indigenous slaves in New England came from the slave network established in South Carolina. This flow of Carolina Indigenous captives from South Carolina and the Spanish Florida slave raids began to filtrate into Rhode Island in 1711.[57] Carolina and Spanish Indigenous slaves continued to be bought and sold in Boston until the 1720s. These captives were held as slaves for decades in Connecticut, Rhode Island, and Massachusetts.[58]

In addition to Indigenous men, women, and children bound as slaves in New England, thousands of African slaves lived and died in the northern colonies.[59] Both Massachusetts and Rhode

Figure 3.9 Illustration of Ticumua people cultivating their crops in North Central Florida. (Pieter van der Aa, *Native Americans planting crops*, 1706, engraving, 13.6 x 17.8 cm (5.4 x 7 in). Courtesy of the John Carter Brown Library.)

Island sponsored voyages carrying rum, staple food items, and manufactured goods from around the Atlantic to Africa in order to procure slaves.[60] Once purchased, African men, women, and children were carried to the West Indies, the southern colonies, and then New England to be sold.[61] Most often, children were sold at New England ports at the end of a slave voyage after the adults were sold in the Caribbean and the southern colonies.[62] By 1730, nearly every major New England port was involved in the African slave trade.[63] Similar to the southern colonies, New England officials began separating Indigenous and African individuals according to who was categorized a slave and who was not. To gain freedom from slavery, the Indigenous people of New England were required to prove they were tied in kinship to a local Native tribe. If men, women, or children were labeled a 'Carolina Indian,' 'Spanish Indian,' 'Mulatto,' or 'Negro,' they would remain slaves for life.[64]

With the rapid increase in the purchase of African labor, 25 percent of the total population in Rhode Island was soon comprised of African slaves.[65] The most concentrated population of African slaves in early 18th century New England was found in the Narragansett region of Rhode Island.[66] The total number of slaves in this area were purchased by gentlemen, merchants, plantation owners, shopkeepers, widows, farmers, and artisans for labor.[67] New England artisans purchased African boys and girls cheaply and then trained them in a skill to assist the artisan with his workload.[68] A census taken in Massachusetts during the mid-18th century revealed the largest slave population resided in Suffolk County, with the highest percentage of African slaves in Boston. Documentation indicates the political and social elite, as well as prominent members of the community and artisans, owned slaves.[69] Rural areas in Massachusetts also saw an increase in African slaves. Deerfield, Massachusetts,

Figure 3.10 Map detailing the close proximity of the West Indies to the colonies. (Thomas Salmon, *West Indies*, 1767, map, 18 x 29 cm (7 x 11 in), Library of Congress.)

Figure 3.11 Rhode Island plantation home of Daniel Cogshell. Initial construction took place in 1725. (Historic American Buildings Survey, *Boston Neck Road State Route 138, Saunderstown, Washington County, RI*, 1933, photograph, Library of Congress.)

possessed a sizable slave population in the mid-18th century.[70] African boys and men were involved in farming, while slave women and girls worked in households engaged in manufacturing cloth and clothing.[71]

TEXTILES AND TEXTILE PRODUCTION

TEXTILES AND SLAVERY

From the beginning of the African slave trade, textiles played a major role in the buying and selling of African men, women, and children into a life of bondage. As mentioned previously, European slave traders paid African rulers with hand-painted, colorful cotton fabrics produced in India for approval to hunt for slaves in specific regions of Africa.[72] In 1727, European traders exported 30 million yards of fabric created in India. The specialty cotton fabrics only India could produce clothed people around the world as well as purchased millions of African slaves.[73] Since the 16th century, India had been known for producing lightweight cotton fabrics decorated in rich colors and interesting motifs. India dyers developed a technique to paint and print their cottons in a rainbow of colors that resisted fading when the fabrics were washed. These textiles became known as chintz or calicos.[74] The world could not get enough of these one-of-a-kind fabrics, including African leaders and merchants.[75]

Figure 3.12 The Allen House located in Deerfield, Massachusetts. Initial construction took place in 1734. (Historic American Buildings Survey, *Allen House, Bars Road, Deerfield, Franklin County MA.*, 1933, photograph, Library of Congress.)

Another type of cotton fabric produced in India and used for the purchase of African captives was a checked cotton known as cherryderry.[76] In early 18th century England, textile manufacturing companies could not reproduce the beautifully patterned and printed cottons of India. However, English weavers could produce a checked cotton similar to the checked cottons of India. The manufacture of cotton checks in Britain provided a way for English traders to compete with European traders in the African slave network. English checked fabrics were used to barter with West African rulers for slaves who could then be sold to colonial plantations.[77] A cheaper version of this checked cotton fabric was used in early America to clothe slaves, as documented in newspaper advertisements detailing the apparel of runaways.[78] A type of checked fabric was also seen in the clothing of slave traders and the captives they were transporting in the 18th century. An eyewitness account of the African slave trade detailed Scottish slave traders dressed in checked shirts. This same checked fabric was also seen on the bodies of the captives in their possession.[79]

Among New England slave narratives of the first half of the 18th century, Venture Smith and James Albert Ukawsaw Gronniosaw recall being purchased with textiles as young children sold into slavery.[80] In his narrative, Venture Smith describes his capture at the age of six along with his father and those he traveled with while trying to escape an invading army in the region of Africa where they resided. Once captured and processed in a slave trade holding fort in Anomabo, Venture was placed on a small boat and rowed out to meet a

Figure 3.13 Hand-painted 18th-century cotton petticoat panel created in India. (*Petticoat Panel*, third quarter of the 18th century, cotton, painted resist and mordant, dyed, 33 5/8 x 67 1/2 in (85.4 x 171.5 cm), Friends of European Sculpture and Decorative Arts Gifts, 1992. Courtesy of The Metropolitan Museum of Art.)

Figure 3.14 Textile sample of an 18th-century hand-printed chintz created in India for export. (*Fragment of India Chintz*, 18th century, cotton, painted and dyed, 12 x 10 1/4 in (30.5 x 26 cm), gift of Titi Halle, 2010. Courtesy of the Metropolitan Museum of Art.)

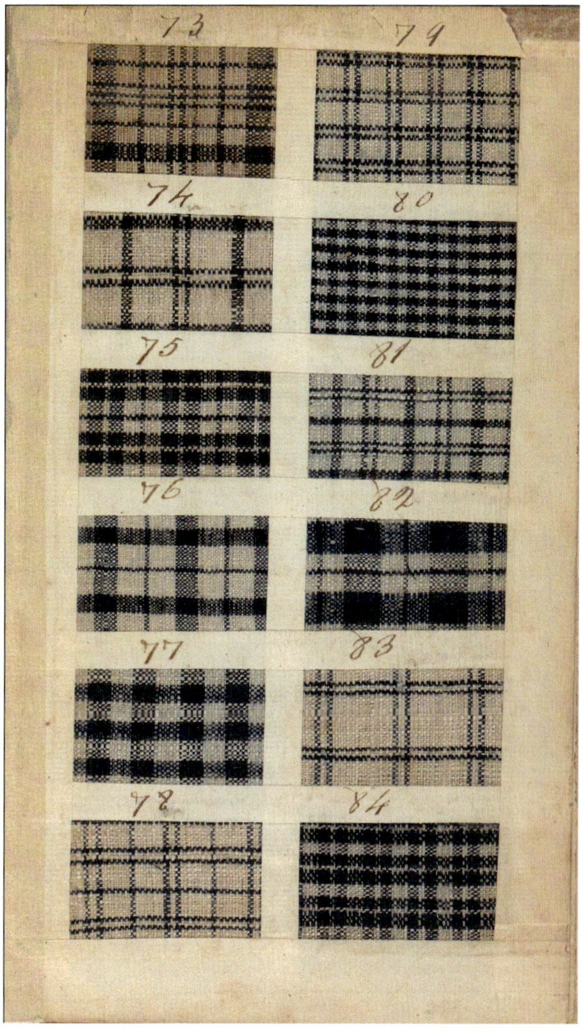

Figure 3.15 18th-century textile sample page of check cotton fabrics produced in Manchester, England, by the textile manufacturing firm of Benjamin and John Bower. (*Textile Sample Book*, Plate 4, 1771, cotton, 8 1/4 x 4 5/8 in (20 x 11.7 cm), Rogers Fund. Image copyright the Metropolitan Museum of Art. Image source: Art Resource, NY.)

Rhode Island slave ship. He was then purchased by the ship's steward, Roberson Mumford, for four gallons of rum and a piece of calico fabric. Venture began his time as a slave in Narragansett, Rhode Island, in the home of Mr. Mumford.[81]

James Albert was born in Bornu in 1710, where he lived with his mother, father, and five siblings. A merchant from the Gold Coast befriended James Albert's parents and convinced them to allow the young boy to travel to the West African colony with the merchant for a visit. The merchant promised to supervise James Albert personally for a time in order to show James wondrous sights, as well as introduce him to the merchant's own sons, who were about the same age. Soon after James Albert arrived at the Gold Coast, he was sold by the merchant into slavery. In his memoir, James Albert recalls being purchased for two yards of checked fabric on a Dutch ship docked in the harbor. Aboard the Dutch ship, he was then taken to Barbados and sold to a young man from New York by the name of Vanhorn. After a time, James Albert was purchased by New Jersey minister and theologian Theodore Frelinghuysen.[82]

TEXTILE PRODUCTION IN THE COLONIES

Early in the 18th century, word spread to England concerning the large quantities of textiles produced in New England and other colonial settlements. In 1705, Lord Cornbury, Governor of the Province of New York, notified the English Council on Trade and detailed the advancement of woolen cloth manufacture in Long Island and Connecticut. Lord Cornbury saw this sizable scale of production as a threat to the dependence of the colonies on England for their textile needs. He advised for the immediate suspension of textile production in the colonies.[83] In 1715, another report to England referenced the large quantities of kersey, linsey-woolsey, hempen cloth, drugget, linen, and flannel manufactured in the colonies. Production of substantial yardages of cloth in the early 18th century increased and spread throughout New England, New York, Pennsylvania, and Maryland.[84] In communities with a concentrated number of textile artists, cloth production was abundant. In Philadelphia, specialty woven fabrics were created by professional weavers equal to textiles found on English import lists.[85] Virginia also saw an increase in cloth production in connection to an economic depression. Small-scale farmers in Virginia, with the aid of their wives and children, made cloth for their household and personal needs.[86] The cloth woven by farmer's wives and their children to supply the home and their wardrobe was known as 'Virginia cloth.'[87]

Fearing this rapidly growing trend of textile production in the colonies, England enacted a policy in 1718 that forbade the exportation of men with the knowledge and skills associated with the creation of cotton, wool, linen, or silk cloth. Anyone caught planning to bring a skilled textile artisan to the colonies from England was fined 100 pounds and imprisoned for three months. This policy was renewed in 1750 with an extra provision that made it illegal to export wool or silk manufacturing tools from Great Britain or Ireland to the colonies. If caught smuggling textile manufacturing equipment into the colonies, the items were confiscated while the guilty party was fined 200 pounds. To further discourage the immigration of men with textile knowledge, in 1750, anyone found communicating with and encouraging a textile artisan to settle in the colonies was fined 500 pounds and jailed for 12 months.[88] Discouraging male weavers from taking residency in the colonies opened a way for young women living at home to make a small income by weaving low-cost, plain weave fabrics for home and the community.[89] Instead of suppressing textile production, these policies increased production in homes, plantations, and private textile manufacturing networks.

CHILDREN AND TEXTILE PRODUCTION

In answer to the restrictions on textile production England put in place in the early 18th century, a number of colonial leaders specifically encouraged the production of textiles in their communities. Boston officials were particularly interested in using child labor for textile production as early as 1720. An appointed committee was formed to establish a spinning school for poor children who resided in the community almshouse. A donation from a charitable Boston citizen, Daniel Oliver, funded the completion of the first spinning school. The school was outfitted with 20 spinning wheels for the almshouse-impoverished children to learn the art of spinning.[90] Thirty years later, in 1750, an advertisement appeared in the *Boston News Letter* detailing that looms for weaving several types of linen were set up and ready to manufacture cloth in the Linen Manufacture House. At the same time, a gentlemen's organization opened several other spinning schools for all Boston children. Parents who cared for their country were encouraged to send their children to learn the essential and useful art of spinning fibers.[91]

The efforts to train young children in textile production expanded further with the creation of another Boston organization focusing on the poor. The Society for Encouraging Industry and Employing the Poor, created in 1751, arranged a sizable community fundraiser for the construction of an additional manufacturing house. On August 8th, 1753, leaders of the event instructed 300 spinners, some as young as seven or eight, to carry their spinning wheels to the Boston Commons where they could showcase the skills they learned with the aid of the organization. As the young girls spun fibers in neatly organized rows, a group of weavers, wearing garments made from the cloth they handmade, entered the Commons with notable gentlemen of the community. During the spinning demonstration and the procession of weavers, a young male weaver was placed on a central stage where he wove cloth.[92] The event was a success. With the funds raised, the new manufacturing house was built on Long Acre Street and utilized by the Boston community until several years after the Revolutionary War. The house was used for the manufacture of linen cloth, available for purchase by community

Figure 3.16 Child's mid-18th century open-front linen dress embroidered with wool. (*Dress*, mid-18th century, linen and wool, Roger's Fund 1954. Courtesy of The Metropolitan Museum of Art.)

members, as well as a school for teaching children spinning techniques. Families who could afford to buy linen goods from the manufacturing house were clothing their children from cloth created by the yarns spun at the hands of other children in the community.[93]

In addition to Boston, other communities in the early 18th century were combining their efforts to create textiles. In the 1740s, a substantial number of Moravians immigrated to Pennsylvania as part of a mission to bring salvation to the Indigenous people of the colony. The Moravian religious leaders created the Pennsylvania Plan to establish Bethlehem and Nazareth, Pennsylvania, as complementary communities. The settlements were to support the primary goal of missionary work by providing all the necessities of life, including textiles and clothing. Nazareth citizens provided the wool and flax for textile production, while Bethlehem citizens created the cloth. In the Moravian textile system, women along with Indigenous converts prepared the flax and wool for spinning, as well as assisted in the shearing of sheep. Women and young children, who were taught to spin by the age of seven or eight, primarily did the spinning.[94] Weaving was organized by gender and assigned to the unmarried members of the community. While men were at times involved in the spinning process, most male unmarried citizens wove heavy fabrics in the Brethren's House where they resided. Single women of the community wove the lighter fabrics in the Sisters' House. As textile production grew, a fulling mill and a large dye house were constructed to expand wool cloth production and finishing in 1751. The industrious textile production activity of the Moravian colonists continued until the early 1760s.[95]

Figure 3.17 Illustration of the Moravian community located in Bethlehem, Pennsylvania. (Paul Sandby and Thomas Pownall, *A view of Bethlehem, the great Moravian settlement in the province of Pennsylvania*, 1761, etching, Library of Congress.)

Figure 3.18 The Brethren's House originally built in 1748. (Historic American Buildings Survey, *Single Brethren's House, 89 West Church Street, Bethlehem, Northampton County, PA.*, 1933, photograph, Library of Congress.)

Figure 3.19 The Sisters' House where spinning and weaving of lightweight fabrics took place in the 18th century. (Historic American Buildings Survey, *Single Sisters' House, 44 West Church Street, Bethlehem, Northampton County, PA.*, 1933, photograph, Library of Congress.)

Figure 3.20 The Shaker loom room located in the Shaker community of New Lebanon, New York. The room houses two 18th-century looms and a walking wheel. (W F Winter, Historic American Buildings Survey, *Shaker South Family, Loom Room, Shaker Road, New Lebanon, Columbia County, NY.*, 1933, photograph, Library of Congress.)

Figure 3.21 Illustration detailing the silk-production process in the 19th century. The woman in the illustration is reeling silk fibers. (Albert Berhause, *How Corticelli silk is made*, 1878–1880, wood engraving, Library of Congress.)

TEXTILES IN THE COLONIES

On several South Carolina plantations, a focused effort to raise silkworms for the creation of silk textiles was underway by the turn of the 18th century. One such plantation went by the name of 'Silk Hope,' and was established by Sir Nathan Johnson.[96] A combination of white indentured workers and Indigenous and African slave labor, was used in raising, feeding, and reeling the fibers from cocoons spun by silkworms. The process of obtaining silk fibers was done in a specially constructed building known as a filature.[97] The filature housed the silkworms, hot water basins, and wooden reeling machines. Slave children were given the responsibility of feeding the silkworms mulberry leaves, while adult workers drew silk fibers from the cocoons. The silk fibers loosened from cocoons as they were placed in hot water. In the fiber drawing process, it took a number of cocoons to create a single thread of silk. After the silk threads were formed, they were stretched out to dry before winding them into a skein in preparation for weaving. Processed silk threads could be woven together with wool in South Carolina to create drugget cloth that combined the durability of wool with the softness of silk.[98] Drugget cloth was primarily used to make heavy coats as well as petticoats.[99]

Due to successful textile production in the early 1700s, a variety of fabrics were available to the growing colonial communities. In New England, weavers like Christopher Leffingwell were creating linens and wools in a number of different weights from fancy linens to fine woolens woven with plain, striped, or patterned surfaces.[100] The community of Bethlehem, Pennsylvania, was known for fine linens as well as their blue and checked woolens.[101] In addition to linens, woolens, and mixed cloth fabrics, colonists in Philadelphia could purchase calamanco, camlet, russels, and a worsted plush cloth.[102] With their connections to the global tobacco trade, wealthy Virginia plantation owners had access to many fine imported fabrics along with homespun fabrics that were produced either directly on their plantations or provided by the local working class.[103]

Wills and inventories of the elite listed nine varieties of silks used in clothing, as well as satin, brocade, and velvet, in addition to silk mixed with wool or flax.[104] Elegant clothing fabrics for Virginia planters came in a number of floral patterns, striped, or plain with trimmings in gold and silver.[105] Woolens were also popular in Virginia wardrobes. A large quantity of broadcloth garments were recorded for the well-to-do, as well as many items made from calamanco.[106] Calamanco was

Figure 3.22 A calamanco quilt made of wool and cotton. (*Wholecloth calamanco quilt*, 1750, wool and cotton, 102 1/2 x 99 1/2 in (260.4 x 252.7 cm), Rogers Fund, 1945. Courtesy of The Metropolitan Museum of Art.)

a thin, decorative, glazed fabric made of worsted wool and imported from England. Popular kinds of calamanco were created with a satin weave, damask weave, or brocaded in floral, stripe, and check designs. It was used in gowns, petticoats, waistcoats, and shoes.[107] Colors were also used to delineate social class in Virginia. The wealthy population could be seen in popular shades of sky blue, sea green, olive, prunella, and scarlet. Due to Virginia's sumptuary laws, only the upper class or their house slaves could wear clothing made of expensive fabrics in bright colors.[108]

In contrast to textiles worn by the wealthy colonial population, the Negro Act of 1735 gives us a glimpse into the fabrics specifically used for clothing slaves. South Carolina's Negro Act of 1735 used legal means to visually separate slaves from other members of the community. Adult and child slaves, either of African or Indigenous descent, could not wear fabrics deemed above their social assignment in the plantation system. The only cloth that slaves could wear, according to the law, was the cheapest and the most coarse available. The list of approved fabrics included duffles, coarse kerseys, osnaburg, blue linen, check linen, coarse garlix, calicos, checked cottons, Scottish plaids, and Negro cloth. The term 'Negro cloth' or 'Slave cloth' was a term used by slave owners to describe rough and cheaply made fabrics that were unfinished.[109] The most common fabrics used in the early 18th century for slave clothing were coarse versions of osnaburg, linsey-woolsey, and kersey.[110]

COLORING TEXTILES IN THE COLONIES

One of the processes used in early textile production was dyeing fibers to bring color to natural or bleached woven cloth. Dyeing practices were

Figure 3.23 Samples of 19th-century Negro cloth created and sold by the Peace Dale Manufacturing Company located in South Kingstown, Rhode Island. The wool-manufacturing company was established by Rowland Hazard I in 1802. These fabric samples were included in a letter written by his son Rowland G. Hazard to his brother Isaac P. Hazard in 1835. (*Rowland G. Hazard letter to I. P. Hazard*, February 25th, 1835, fabric samples, Object no. RHi X17 3595E. Courtesy of the Rhode Island Historical Society.)

simple in early colonial homes and then expanded to include more complex techniques as textile production increased. In homes where dyeing fibers took place, an earthenware dye pot was placed in the chimney corner just inside the fireplace. The pot was covered with a piece of board where children often sat during the day to watch over the dyeing process. Home dyes were often made of indigo and dissolved in urine. Spun yarn was placed in the pot until it absorbed the amount of color desired.[111] In addition to indigo, colonists experimented with native berries, flowers, nuts, vegetables, leaves, stems, bark, and roots to bring color to their homespun cloth.[112] The practice of using natural elements to dye cloth in the colonial home was similar to the techniques used by Indigenous people of the region.

Indigenous women gathered plants, roots, and strips of bark, which were then crushed and soaked in water during the dye preparation process. Urine, salt, raw alum, ashes, iron, or copper were used as mordants. A mordant attached to the molecules of a fiber, just as the dye attached to the mordant. The use of a mordant bound the dye to the fiber to ensure the dye remained colorfast.[113] When the crushed powder, water, and mordant mixture was ready in the dye pot, fibers were placed in the concoction that was brought to a boil by using heated stones or a fire pit. Fibers were stirred as they heated to make sure the color took evenly during the dyeing process. In the Indigenous dye method, fibers were most often dyed before they were hand spun. The heating time of the fiber in the dye mixture depended on the tint desired and the color strength of the organic material used to produce the color.[114]

During colonial textile production, the dyeing process was approached in a variety of ways. Dyeing could take place before the fibers were spun, after the fibers were spun into yarn, or after the cloth was made. If dyeing was not done in the home, a weaver could dye the spun yarn before it was woven into cloth.[115] If a weaver did not have the time or skills to dye the wool yarn before the weaving process, the finished cloth was sent to the fulling mill where dyeing was often part of the finishing process. Fulling was the process of cleansing and thickening cloth after it was woven.[116] To create fulled fabric, the cloth was washed, shrunk, and felted. After the felting process, the nap of the cloth was raised by brushing the surface with the head of dried teasel flowers. The hook of the dried teasels

Figure 3.24 Fireplace in a small Rhode Island home. Initial construction took place in 1700.

(George J. Vailliancourt, Historic American Buildings Survey, *Fireplace House, Entrance "A" Road to Lincoln Woods Reservation, Saylesville, Providence County, RI.*, 1933, photograph, Library of Congress.)

pulled the fibers of the cloth up without breaking the fibers. Once the nap had risen, a shearman cut the nap to an equal height to create a nicely finished fabric. Fulling mills, with an attached dye house, could also dye the cloth during the fulling process.[117] For customers who could afford the cost of fulled fabric, the finished woolen cloth for men's attire was referred to as 'fulled cloth.'[118] 'Pressed cloth' was a woman's woolen fabric prepared by a weaver and sent to a fulling mill to complete. The finishing process for women's woolen cloth was less intensive. When a weaver completed the woolen fabric, the 'pressed cloth' was fulled, simply dyed, and pressed by the fulling mill workers.[119]

In addition to dyeing textiles in the home, at the weaver's, or in a fulling mill, professional fabric dyers and printers were setting up shops in larger cities by the early 18th century. Printing on fabric could be done in the home or in a professional printer's shop. In the home, simple patterns were carved into wooden blocks or carved blocks could be borrowed or purchased. A red dye made from madder root, or a blue dye made from the indigo plant were the most common colors used in the early colonial fabric printing process. In the simplest printing technique, the organic dye elements were combined with a mordant in order to adhere the color mixture to the block as well as bind it to the fabric. Alum, salt, chrome, copper, iron, tannic acid, and tin were used as mordants in the colonial printing process. After the block was dipped in the thickened dye

Figure 3.25 Illustration of the indigo plant. (Benedetto Bordiga, *L'Incaco*, 1791, engraving, 17.6 x 11.3 cm (6.9 x 4.4 in). Courtesy of the John Carter Brown Library.)

Figure 3.26 Photograph of an early 19th-century dye house. (Historic American Buildings Survey, *Rappite Dye House, Main & Granary Streets, New Harmony, Posey County, IN.*, 1933, photograph, Library of Congress.)

and mordant base, the home printer could press the block against the fabric, steadily working her way down the length or width of the cloth.[120] In a professional fabric printer's shop, the process could be more complex. Multiple layers of color and pattern could be added to a stretched piece of cloth after each layer of printing dried. Instead of printing with a thickened dye and mordant mixture on a wooden block, the printer could also stamp the fabric with a thickened mordant base that attracted dye to the fibers. Once the mordant mixture was stamped on the fabric, the fabric was then placed into a prepared dye bath. The printed mordant on the fabric would react to the dye bath differently than the areas of the cloth that were not stamped.[121]

In Boston, beginning in 1720, at least nine professional craftsmen with experience in dyeing or printing were offering their skills to the community through advertisements in the local newspapers.[122] An unknown fabric printer placed one of the earliest advertisements in the *Boston Gazette* from April 18th through to April 25th of 1720. The printer claimed to be able to print linens, calico, and silk with durable colors. In 1735, a calico printer by the name of Francis Gray, from Holland, advertised in the *Boston Gazette* that he could print all sorts of calicos in several colors.[123] The term 'calico' referred to his ability to hand stamp cotton cloth in a variety of colors and patterns.[124] Alexander Fleming, from Great Britain, could dye wool, silk, and linen. In his advertisement

Figure 3.27 Textile sample of the block print pattern found on the 18th-century child's dress in Figure 2.30 Photograph taken by the author. Courtesy of Historic New England.

on May 14th, 1754, in the *Boston Gazette*, Fleming listed his ability to dye scarlet, crimson, pink, purple, straw, wine colors, sea green, yellows, and blues. Advertisements for dyers were also seen in Philadelphia. Michael Brown was the first dyer to place an ad in the *Pennsylvania* Gazette, on July 7th, 1737. Brown worked as a dyer of silk, cotton, and linen until his death in the 1750s.[125] Likewise, in Virginia, William Dubberly placed an ad in the *Virginia Gazette* on July 8th, 1737, announcing not only his skills as a hatter, but his ability to dye silk, wool, and woolen fabrics at a reasonable cost. To dye the brighter colors sought after in Virginia, professional dyers used dyes shipped from England to the colonies. These expensive dyes could be found in Virginia stores where English imports were sold. Listed among the colorful dye supplies available in Virginia for purchase were cochineal, fustic, indigo, logwood, madder, turmeric, brazilwood, and walnut.[126]

Indigo was one of the most sought-after dyes in the colony due to the fact it could color every type of textile.[127] Before 1745, some indigo was home grown, but most of the dye was imported on British ships by way of trade with France and Spain. War between Britain and Spain from 1739 to 1748, over control of trade with the American colonies, caused an economic depression felt by South Carolina's rice plantation system. In order to survive the depression, South Carolina families had to find another way to make a profit.[128] George Lucas, a British Army officer, moved his family from Antigua Island to South Carolina in 1738. They settled in what became known as Wappoo Plantation located in close proximity to Wappoo Creek near Albemarle Point. Lucas was commissioned in

Figure 3.28 Front view of a woman's bodice made from a multi-color, hand-printed calico dated 1774. (*Dress*, 1774, cotton and linen, gift of Helen Macartney, 1926. Courtesy of The Metropolitan Museum of Art.)

1739 to leave his family in South Carolina and travel back to his military post in Antigua. While stationed in the West Indies, Lucas began sending his 17-year-old daughter, Eliza, seeds to grow on his plantation to evaluate what crop might bring the Lucas family out of economic depression. By 1740, Eliza was experimenting with indigo seeds her father had sent. The first few years of growing indigo plants for Eliza were not successful. Patience and perseverance paid off, however, when, in 1744, Eliza's experiments and the work of a master dyer, Patrick Cromwell, proved to England that Carolina land could produce indigo dye comparable to France's.[129]

By 1745, the Lucas family began reaping the financial rewards for their production of indigo. With the success of Wappoo Plantation, other South Carolina plantation owners, with the labor of their slaves, began growing indigo for export as well. In 1747, over 135,000 pounds of indigo were produced and prepared for export.[130] The indigo crop became invaluable to South Carolina's economy. Due to the continuing war, Britain's access to Europe's indigo trade was cut off and Carolina stepped in as the new supplier of indigo. Again, in 1757, during the Seven Years War, Carolina planters saw an opportunity for profit by producing 876,400 pounds of indigo for exportation.[131] With the newfound success of producing large quantities of indigo in the colonies, the fashionable blue dye was made readily available to other colonial communities. A blue resist print technique on cloth became quite popular with the increase in indigo availability. This discharge print method used two shades of indigo on a linen or cotton and linen mixed fabric. A common blue resist print was

Figure 3.29 Image of the Sinkler plantation built by a family of indigo planters. Initial construction took place in 1808. (Frances Benjamin Johnston, *Eutaw, Eutawville vic., Berkeley County, South Carolina*, 1938, photograph, Library of Congress.)

Figure 3.30 Textile sample of the popular blue resist technique of the mid-18th century. (*Curtain panel, blue resist textile*, 1725–1775, cotton, painted and block printed resist, dyed, 59 5/8 x 78 3/16 in (151.4 x 198.6 cm), Rogers Fund, 1940. Courtesy of The Metropolitan Museum of Art.)

Figure 3.31 Child's indigo-printed 18th-century linen coat. (*Coat*, third quarter of the 18th century, linen, gift of Mrs. Alice Raphael, 1937. Courtesy of The Metropolitan Museum of Art.)

composed of leaves and birds stamped on a natural color or bleached background. On May 7th, 1759, in the *Boston Gazette*, linen printer and dyer John Hickey, of Dublin, Ireland, advertised his experience in blue and white fabric printing.[132]

CLOTHING

INDIGENOUS COMMUNITIES AND ANGLO-EUROPEAN CLOTHING

English garments began to filter into Indigenous clothing and language in the late 17th and early 18th centuries. By 1709, along the Atlantic coast, the Indigenous language included words for dress, English shirt, pair of breeches, coat, shoes, and neckcloth. In probate inventories of New England's Indigenous settlements in Natick, Nantucket, and Chilmark, a mixture of English clothing items and Native garments were listed as personal belongings.[133] Indigenous men of all ages wore British great coats, quilted coats, jackets, shirts, gloves, and belts. Women and older girls possessed gowns, shifts, shirts, aprons, pocket cases, petticoats, and stays.[134] The introduction of cotton cloth in gingham and calico prints to the Indigenous population created a shift in female clothing. Indigenous-style dresses first appeared in cotton cloth, followed by dresses similar in style to European fashion.[135] From early 18th century records and documented personal accounts, a mixture of English and Indigenous clothing items was worn together.[136] Indigenous clothing items most worn with English-style garments were skin leggings, moccasins, blankets, and mantles. Within this mix of British and Native clothing, the Indigenous people of colonial New England were documented to prefer a variety of colorful garments. Red was a particularly favorite color in the early 18th century.[137] Naomi Ommaush, an Indigenous woman of Aquinnah, Massachusetts, left a blue calico dress, a petticoat, and a red coat to her relatives upon her death.[138]

Indigenous people of Pennsylvania who worked and lived among the Moravian communities of Bethlehem and Nazareth also began adopting English-style clothing into their wardrobes.[139] Reverend John Wesley, upon his arrival to Georgia in 1736, recorded his first meeting with Chief Tomochichi and three of his men. Wesley described the members of the Yamacraw tribe wearing European clothing. In addition to wearing European clothing pieces, Chief Tomochichi painted his face for this first encounter as well as adorned his hair with beads and attached a scarlet feather to one ear.[140] Captive Indigenous men, women, and children sold to colonists were also clothed in English and European clothing items. Once an Indigenous captive was purchased and claimed by their owners, they were disrobed of their traditional clothing and given simple English or European garments to wear. Advertisements detailing the escape of Indigenous servants in the colonies commonly detailed the English clothing they were wearing at the time of their disappearance.[141] John Pittme, an Indigenous servant, ran away from his Boston master in 1739 wearing a gray coat with pewter buttons, leather breeches, and a tow shirt.[142]

AFRICAN ENSLAVED CLOTHING

English traveler William Hugh Grove traveled on a ship carrying African captives from Bristol,

Figure 3.32 Portrait of Chief Cunne Shote dressed in a combination of European and Cherokee traditional clothing. (John McArdell, *Cunne Shote, the Indian chief, a great warrior of the Cherokee nation*, 1762, mezzotint engraving, 30.8 x 25.1 cm (12 x 10 in). Courtesy of the John Carter Brown Library.)

England, to Yorktown, Virginia, in 1732. Mr. Grove documented in his personal journal that the African children on board had no clothing, neither did a large number of men and women. Men and women, who had some semblance of clothing, relied on a small rag or piece of leather to cover their lower anatomy. Once the ship docked, purchased men and women were given coarse clothing to wear by their owners. From Grove's description, the men were placed in shirts and 'drawers,' which were a simple style of breeches.[143] Fabric for clothing slaves was not only made on the local level in the colonies, but large quantities of coarse osnaburg were also imported from Scotland and Germany.[144] An unusual fabric approved for slaves to wear in the Negro Act of 1735, among the listing of coarse cloths, was Scottish plaid. When examining the historical events surrounding the Battle of Culloden, along with the large migration of Scottish immigrants to the colonies, Scottish plaid became more readily available in the mid-18th century. Colonial Scottish slavers or Scottish families purchasing slaves for labor could easily have used tartan to clothe African men, women, and older children.[145]

John Woolman, an 18th-century merchant, tailor, journalist, Quaker preacher, and early abolitionist, often referred to the lowly state of slave clothing. In his personal journal and powerful anti-slavery publication, *Some Considerations On The Keeping of Negros*, Woolman commented that adult African male and female slaves hardly had clothes to cover their nakedness. He also observed that ten and 12-year-old boys and girls were given very little clothing in contrast to the children of the slave masters. He described the clothing given to slaves as 'uncomely garments' that were coarse and ragged.[146] Outer garments and under garments for the slave population were often made from rough fabrics that were uncomfortable for the wearer.[147] The profit-minded slave owner clothed enslaved African men, women, and

Figure 3.33 Illustration of Scottish soldiers in their tartan kilts and caps in the 17th century. (G. Köler, *Kurtze Beschreibung, dess auss Irrland, Königl. Majestat in Schweden ankommenten Volcks von dero Lands Art, Natur, Waffen vnnd Eigenschafft In solchem Habit gehen die 800 in Stettin angekommen Irrländer oder Irren*, 1631, engraving with letterpress, 39 x 28 cm (15 x 11 in), Library of Congress.)

children in the bare minimum. South Carolina slave children were often inadequately dressed in poorly made coarse garments.[148] Savilla Burrell, a South Carolina slave, describes in her narrative what little clothing they were given to wear. Grown boys in the summer were only given a long shirt to wear with no shoes.[149] Ellen Swindler, a child slave from South Carolina, detailed she had one dress, a pair of shoes, and at times, one change of clothing.[150] In an effort to visually portray slaves as paid workers rather than owned property, some adult slave clothing in the colonial south was reminiscent of garments worn by English farmers.[151] In his travel journal, William Hugh Grove documented that slave owners he associated with gave male slaves a yearly allowance of ten yards of brown linen, which could produce two shirts and two pairs of pants. This was in addition to one pair of shoes.[152]

When it came to making clothing for slaves, colonial Virginia records indicate women of large estates were often responsible for overseeing garments constructed for family members as well as the household servants and slaves.[153] Mistresses of these sizable estates relied on assistance from paid help, slaves, servants, and their daughters to create textiles and clothing.[154] The process of making textiles and clothes for those living on a plantation was documented in South Carolina and Georgia. Jessie Sparrow, an enslaved man in South Carolina, recorded in his personal slave narrative that his mother, Sally Bowens, was a slave seamstress who cut and made all the plantation clothing. As a young child, Sally was taken from her mother to be

Figure 3.34 Image of 18th-century slave quarters and summer kitchen located on the Piper Farm in Sharpsburg, Maryland. (Historic American Buildings Survey, *Piper Farm, Slave Quarters, Sharpsburg, Washington County, MD.*, 1933 photograph, Library of Congress.)

Figure 3.35 Portrait of Mrs. William Byrd II with an enslaved boy standing behind her dressed in blue livery. (Lucy Parke Byrd (Mrs. William Byrd II), 1716, oil on canvas, 50 x 40 in (127 x 101.6 cm). Courtesy of the Virginia Museum of History and Culture.)

raised by the plantation mistress. Under the instruction of the mistress, Sally became a house slave who was later trained to make clothing for the plantation population.[155] In Georgia, Annie Huff and her daughters were given the tasks of carding, spinning, and knitting to help produce clothing for the plantation on which they were enslaved.[156] If enslaved women and young girls were required to work in the fields during the day, their textile and clothing production duties took place after sunset.[157] When the production of clothing was not overseen by a plantation mistress, slaves were given an allowance of cloth each year to make their own garments, in addition to their assigned work.[158]

Many wealthy Virginia plantation owners who wished to showcase their English coat of arms, clothed their house slaves in livery, while their field slaves wore minimal clothing.[159] Special livery could be ordered directly from London without going through a Virginia merchant. Soon after his marriage to Martha Custis, George Washington sent a clothing order to London for a slave boy who had been given to his eight-year-old stepson. The 14-year-old enslaved boy's primary responsibility was to wait on young John Park Custis. In the order to London, Washington requested three pairs of shoes, three pairs of stockings, and a suit of livery designed to reflect the coat of arms designated to the Custis family.[160] In 1735, soon after the Negro Act of South Carolina passed, merchants in Charleston began to advertise ready-made slave clothing. The garments produced and sold were meant to clothe both Indigenous and African slaves.[161] In contrast to the subtle earth tone colors of homespun clothing for slaves, the ready-made jackets, breeches, loose-fitting trousers, coarse

Figure 3.36 Portrait of George Washington's stepchildren, John and Martha Parke Custis. (John Wollaston, *Portrait of John and Martha Parke Custis*, 1757, oil on canvas, 50 x 40 in (127 x 1016 cm). Courtesy of Museums at Washington and Lee University.)

stockings, and caps came in a variety of colors.[162] The items were available in white, blue, green, and red. By 1747, with the large production of indigo, slave clothing sold and worn by African and Indigenous captives was available in solid blue, blue stripes, or blue checks.[163] In addition to selling everyday common dress for South Carolina slave men and boys, livery could be ordered and imported to a colonial merchant's shop.[164]

ANGLO-EUROPEAN UPPER-CLASS CHILDREN'S CLOTHING

In contrast to the clothing worn by Indigenous and African children, were garments worn by children of affluent families. When George Washington placed the livery order for his stepson's personal slave, he also purchased clothing for both of his stepchildren. For his stepson, John Parke, Washington ordered a suit for winter, a suit for summer, six pairs of fine cotton stockings, one pair of worsted wool stockings, four pairs of sturdy shoes, one pair of heeled shoes, one pair of gloves, a pair of shoe and knee buckles, and a pair of sleeve buttons. For his six-year-old stepdaughter, Martha Parke, Washington ordered a silk coat, a bib apron, four lawn dresses, two cambric frocks, a satin hooded cloak, a Persian quilted coat, a pair of pack thread stays, six pairs of leather shoes, two pairs of satin shoes, six pairs of fine cotton stockings, four pairs of white worsted stockings, six pairs of white kid gloves, a pair of silver shoe buckles, and a pair of sleeve buttons.[165]

The children of Upper-class Virginians in the early 18th century dressed similarly to the children of gentry in southwestern England. Many of the first families of Virginia emigrated from southwestern England and brought their taste in European fashion with them.[166] Distinction of class through clothing was an integral part of colonial Virginia. Early Virginia sumptuary laws were specifically created to keep community members from dressing above their social class.[167] As seen with the Custis children, wealthy children possessed many clothing items made in a variety of expensive fabrics. A boy's wardrobe from a wealthy home could consist of a dozen shirts, eight cravats, six waistcoats, a variety of colored stockings, six pairs of breeches, a variety of hats, and several pairs of gloves. A young girl could have as many as a dozen gowns made in a variety of fine fabrics, petticoats, an under hoop, two aprons, a cloak, one good pair of stays, six pairs of shoes, a dozen pair of stockings in cotton and wool, and ten pairs of gloves.[168]

ANGLO-EUROPEAN BOYS' CLOTHING

Boys in the early 18th century seemed to have gone through three stages of dress. The youngest

Figure 3.37 Portrait of the three-year-old James Badger, painted in a tight-fitted bodice resembling a man's coat attached to a full skirt with an open front to reveal the under petticoat. (Joseph Badger, *James Badger*, 1760, oil on canvas, 42 1/2 x 33 1/8 in (108 x 84.1 cm), Rogers Fund, 1929. Courtesy of the Metropolitan Museum of Art.)

Figure 3.38 A pair of boy's breeches originally worn by C. Tuill in 1758. The breeches were also worn by C. Tuill's son and grandchildren. (Pair of boy's breeches, 1758, cotton and silk plain weave, 45 x 43 cm (17 11/16 x 16 15/16 in). Courtesy of the Museum of Fine Arts, Boston.)

boys were dressed in simple gowns similar to long frilled shirts, with a long full coat placed over the gown for warmth. In the next stage, before they were breeched, boys were often seen in petticoats with a variety of over garments that combined both feminine and masculine elements. Male children in this period have been painted in tight-fitted bodices that resemble a masculine coat attached to full skirts, or more feminine garments resembling a gown worn by their sisters. Some of the skirts were depicted by artists as full skirts with no front opening, while other skirts seem to be less full with a front opening to reveal the petticoat underneath.[169] Another over garment detailed in this second stage of dress was a fitted coat with skirts that reached to the ankle. These coats were often tied at the waist with a sash.[170] The third stage of dress, like the painting of John Parke Custis, placed boys by the age of seven into clothing similar to adult men. At this stage, boys were clothed in long tail shirts with ruffle collars and sleeves, long waistcoats, knee breeches, stockings, and suit frock coats.[171]

In the portrait of the Grymes children, painted by John Wollaston, there are three boys of different ages captured in the family portrait. Charles, the youngest boy of toddler age, is wearing a simple gown with a ruffled neck and gathered sleeves that end in another ruffle. John is just a few years older and has not been breeched. He is wearing a red dress with a fitted bodice that has been trimmed in lace and buttons to resemble a man's military coat. Under his full-skirted dress, John is clothed in a high neck chemise with a ruffled collar and sleeves. Over the red dress, John is painted in a long, dark

Figure 3.39 Portrait of Lucy, John Randolph, Phillip Ludwell, and Charles Grymes. (Gustavus Hesselius, *Portrait of the children of Philip and Mary Grymes of Middlesex, County, 1750–1755*, oil on canvas, 56 x 66 in (142.24 x 167.64 cm). Courtesy of the Virginia Museum of History and Culture.)

blue coat with fitted sleeves. The oldest brother, Phillip, is clothed in a brown ditto suit with a full-skirted frock coat and knee breeches. To coordinate with his suit, Phillip is wearing a silver-embroidered waistcoat, and a shirt ending in sleeve ruffles. The last piece of Phillip's clothing is a cravat tied around his neck as his father would have worn. Boys wore cravats with their suits from the time they were breeched through to their adulthood.[172]

In contrast to wealthy children of Virginia, Massachusetts children's clothing was confined to kersey, linsey-woolsey, serges, and druggets made of wool. The simple dress of Virginia servants was more similar to homespun New England clothing than the clothing of Virginia's elite. In New England, wool, often combined with flax or tow, was used as the outwear for a majority of the population in cold weather. Hempen cloth and linen, from coarse to the finest osnaburg or Holland, were the principal fabrics for outerwear and under garments during warmer seasons.[173] Homes provided plaid or striped linen under garments in New England regardless of social class.[174] Beginning in 1718, another flood of experienced Irish textile workers immigrating to Massachusetts was the catalyst for an increase in linen production. Superior linens in browns, speckled, striped, and checked patterns added more variety to the New England wardrobe.[175]

ANGLO-EUROPEAN GIRLS' CLOTHING

Smaller girls wore simple dresses with bodices that laced up the back, similar to the dress worn

Figure 3.40 A pair of 18th-century brown-stripe homespun boy's breeches. (*Homespun breeches*, 18th century, waist 14 x outseam 15 in (waist 35.56 x outseam 38 cm). Courtesy of Old Sturbridge Village, Sturbridge, Massachusetts.)

by Martha Parke Custis in the painting by John Wollaston.[176] Under the gray silk gown, Martha is clothed in a chemise, a petticoat, and a pair of stays. Packthread stays were a more flexible variety of stays worn by children.[177] Martha's silk sleeves are fitted and end in a ruffle that has been attached to the bottom edge of the sleeve. Below the ruffle of the gown sleeve, John Wollaston depicted a ruffled end to the sleeve of the chemise Martha is wearing underneath. Older girls, by the age of 12, often wore a more complicated split front, robe-style gown called a mantua, comparable to those worn by adult women.[178] The mantua was open at the bodice to reveal a stomacher, which was pinned to a pair of more rigid stays worn underneath the gown. The split continued down the front of the gown to showcase an elaborate petticoat.[179] Petticoats for Upper class women and girls in the early 18th century were made of rich fabrics and often elaborately decorated. By 1738, colonial female mantua makers began advertising their skills in creating gowns as fashionable as those in London for the wealthy female population.[180]

In the portrait of the Grymes children, Lucy is not painted in a mantua but rather in a blue silk gown with a long-pointed bodice over her stays. A white apron bib, edged in lace, has been placed over the bodice. The shape of the bib mimics the shape of a woman's stomacher of the time. The sleeves of the gown are gathered or finely pleated at the top of the bodice and end in a cuff that has been pleated in front to curve with the bend of the elbow. Lucy is also wearing a chemise underneath her gown, which is seen at the edge of the bodice neck as well as the edge of the sleeve cuff. The gathered sleeve of the chemise created

Figure 3.41 Woman's hand-painted silk mantua. The robe-style dress is open to reveal a stomacher and elaborate petticoat. (*Robe á la Française*, Britain, 1740, silk, pigment, linen, Harris Brisbane Dick Fund, 1995. Courtesy of The Metropolitan Museum of Art.)

Figure 3.42 Child's simple ribbed white cotton stomacher with linen tabs and backing found in an early American trunk. (*Child's stomacher*, 18 x 15 cm (7 1/16 x 5 7/8 in), cotton and linen, the Elizabeth Day McCormick Collection. Courtesy of the Museum of Fine Arts, Boston.)

Figure 3.43 Green 18th-century American quilted silk petticoat. (*Petticoat*, 18th century, silk, gift of Mrs. Charles E Strang, 1958. Courtesy of The Metropolitan Museum of Art.)

Figure 3.44 Portrait of Catherina Elmendorf of Kingstown, New York. Catherina was the daughter of Petres Emundus Elmendorf and Mary Crooke. (*Catherina Elmendorf*, 1752, oil on canvas, 50 x 40 in (127 x 101.6 cm), gift of Katharine H. Aldrich, 2006. Courtesy of The Metropolitan Museum of Art.)

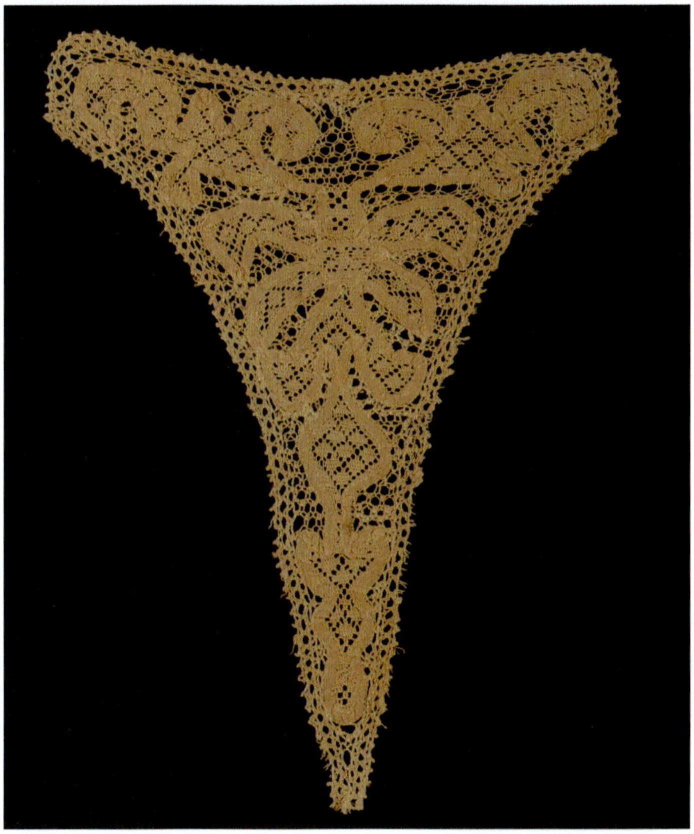

Figure 3.45 Lace stomacher, similar to Catherina's, made from linen in Plymouth Village, Massachusetts, by Barbara Standish for her daughter Loara. (*Lace Stomacher*, 1625–50, 8 x 6 in (20.32 x 15.24 cm). Courtesy of the Pilgrim Hall Museum.)

Figure 3.46 Child's brown bodice with ¾ sleeves attached to a cartridge-pleated skirt. The center front of the bodice lies over the center front of the skirt and is not attached. (*Dress*, Britain, 1740, wool and silk, Poliare Weissman Fund, 1990. Courtesy of The Metropolitan Museum of Art.)

Figure 3.47 Back view of the child's brown dress where leading ties have been attached to the shoulder area of the bodice. (*Dress*, Britain, 1740, wool and silk, Poliare Weissman Fund, 1990. Courtesy of The Metropolitan Museum of Art.)

Figure 3.48 Child's simple purple and white vertically striped linen T-shaped dress with a gored skirt, now faded to brown. The garment has a wide neckline with a small placket center front where a drawstring was tied. (*Dress*, late 18th century, linen, shoulder 7.5, skirt length 21, waist 23 in (shoulder 19, skirt length 53.34, waist 58.42 cm), gift of Mrs. James Bordley Jr., 1951. Courtesy of the Maryland Center for History and Culture.)

the under-ruffle treatment that visually finishes the gown sleeves. The skirt portion of the white apron seems to be tucked under the point of the bodice and folded up to reveal the full skirt of the blue gown. Lucy is likely to be wearing petticoats under her full skirt. It was common for older girls to also wear early types of hoop structures under their gowns, like their mothers.[181] Similar to Lucy Grimes, Catherina Elmendorf is clothed in a gown consisting of a fitted bodice with elbow-length cuffed sleeves, attached to a cartridge pleated skirt. Under the gown, Catherina wears a chemise with a ruffled neck and gathered sleeves that create a ruffle effect under the cuffed sleeves of the bodice. To finish the design of the gown, a cream lace stomacher has been stitched or pinned to the front of the bodice.

The early to mid-18th century saw an increase in the colonial plantation slavery system, textile production, the types of fabrics available in the colonies, and the use of children to create those textiles. Textiles were also used on a substantial scale to purchase and import more African slaves to the colonies. The growth in colonial textile production created opportunities for the exploration of coloring and hand-printing fabrics in a variety of shades and patterns. These techniques could be done in the home or in an artisan's shop. English and European clothing items were becoming more prevalent in Indigenous communities, while enslaved individuals were either dressed in finery or the bare minimum, depending on their position in their master's home. Whether enslaved children were dressed well or only provided with a few coarse garments was the decision of their owner. Children of more established families went through several stages and styles of dress, with each stage of dress taking place at a certain age and linked to gender. Depending on the social status of the colonial child, these styles of dress were either created from expensive fabrics or homespun cloth.

NOTES

1 Robert Bucholz, "Queen Anne: The Most Successful Stuart," *Wondrium Daily*, December 1, 2017, www.wondriumdaily.com/queen-anne-the-most-successful-stuart/.

2 Richard Middleton and Anne Lombard, *Colonial America: A History to 1763*, 4th ed. (West Sussex: Wiley-Blackwell, 2011), 182–86, 197, 202.

3 Daragh Grant, "'Civilizing' the Colonial Subject: The Co-Evolution of State and Slavery in South Carolina, 1670–1739," *Comparative Studies in Society and History* 57, no. 3 (2015): 619, www.jstor.org/stable/43908365.

4 Peter H. Wood, *Black Majority: Negros in Colonial South Carolina From 1670 Through the Stono Rebellion* (New York: W.W. Norton & Company, 1974), 153; M. Eugene Sirmans, "The Legal Status of the Slave in South

Carolina, 1670–1740," *The Journal of Southern History* 28, no. 4 (1962): 471, https://doi.org/10.2307/2205410.

5 Sven Beckert, *Empire of Cotton* (New York: Vintage Books, 2015), 36.

6 Edith Abbott, "A Study of the Early History of Child Labor in America," *American Journal of Sociology* 14, no. 1 (1908): 21, www.jstor.org/stable/2762758.

7 Kathleen A. Staples and Madelyn Shaw, *Clothing Through American History* (Oxford: Greenwood, 2013), 176.

8 Rebecca Anne Goetz, "Rethinking the 'Unthinking Decision': Old Questions and New Problems in the History of Slavery and Race in the Colonial South," *The Journal of Southern History* 75, no. 3 (2009): 605, https://www.jstor.org/stable/27779027.

9 Alan Gallay, *The Indian Slave Trade: The Rise of the English Empire in the American South, 1670–1717* (New Haven: Yale University Press, 2002), 164, 208; Denise I. Bossy, "Godin & Co.: Charleston Merchants and the Indian Trade, 1674–1715," *The South Carolina Historical Magazine* 114, no. 2 (2013): 97, www.jstor.org/stable/23645467.

10 Gallay, *The Indian Slave Trade*, 97.

11 Robbie Ethridge and Sheri M. Shuck-Hall, eds., *Mapping the Mississippian Shatter Zone: The Colonial Indian Slave Trade and Regional Insta* (University of Nebraska Press, 2009), 300, https://doi.org/10.2307/j.ctt1dgn4d8.

12 A. B. Wilkinson, *Blurring the Lines of Race & Freedom: Mulattoes & Mixed Bloods in English Colonial America* (Chapel Hill: University of Nort Carolina Press, 2020), 95.

13 Ethridge and Shuck-Hall, *Mapping the Mississippian Shatter Zone*, 300.

14 Gallay, 189, 200, 201, 211.

15 Gallay, 189, 200, 201, 211.

16 Rodney M. Baine, "Indian Slavery in Colonial Georgia," *The Georgia Historical Quarterly* 79, no. 2 (1995): 419, www.jstor.org/stable/40583244.

17 Ethridge and Shuck-Hall, 300.

18 Gallay, 330.

19 Gallay, 338.

20 Brad Hinshelwood, "The Carolinian Context of John Locke's Theory of Slavery," *Political Theory* 41, no. 4 (2013): 579, http://www.jstor.org/stable/23484595.

21 Gallay, 305.

22 John C. Coombs, "The Phases of Conversion: A New Chronology for the Rise of Slavery in Early Virginia," *The William and Mary Quarterly* 68, no. 3 (2011): 356, https://doi.org/10.5309/willmaryquar.68.3.0332.

23 Ethridge and Shuck-Hall, 299; Joseph Floyd, "Ghosts of Guale: Sugar Houses, Spanish Missions, and the Struggle for Georgia's Colonial Heritage," *The Georgia Historical Quarterly* 97, no. 4 (2013): 389, 392, www.jstor.org/stable/24636327.

24 Baine, "Indian Slavery in Colonial Georgia," 418, 420, 424.

25 Roxanne Dunbar-Ortiz, *An Indigenous Peoples' History of the United States* (Boston: Beacon Press, 2014), 53.

26 Manning Susan et al., eds., *The Edinburgh History of Scottish Literature: Enlightenment, Britain and Empire (1707–1918)* (Edinburgh University Press, 2007), 277, www.jstor.org/stable/10.3366/j.ctt1g09x78.

27 David Hackett Fischer, *Albion's Seed: Four British Folkways in America* (New York: Oxford University Press, 1989), 608.

28 Dunbar-Ortiz, *Indigenous People's History*, 53.

29 Pickney G. McElwee, *Genealogy of William McElwee II, of Clarks Fork of York County, South Carolina* (Waxahachie: G. W. Oates, 1978), 1.

30 David Loranger and Eulanda A. Sanders, "Sumptuary Synergy: British Imperialism Through the Tartan and Slave Trades," *Textile Society of America Symposium Proceedings*, October 2016, 690, Digital Commons@ University of Nebraska-Lincon.

31 Beckert, *Empire of Cotton*, 36.

32 Loranger and Sanders, "Sumptuary Synergy," 686.

33 Loranger and Sanders, 684.

34 Margaret Ellen Newell, *Brethren by Nature: New England Indians, Colonists, and the Origins of American Slavery* (Ithaca: Cornell University Press, 2015), 208.

35 Landers Jane, "Slavery in the Lower South," *OAH Magazine of History* 17, no. 3 (2003): 25, www.jstor.org/stable/25163596.

36 Wood, *Black Majority*, xiv.

37 Newell, *Brethren by Nature*, 208.

38 Wood, 146.

39 Grant, "'Civilizing' the Colonial Subject," 619.

40 Wilkinson, *Blurring the Lines of Race & Freedom*, 21.

41 Wilkinson, 21.

42 Wood, 153; M. Eugene Sirmans, "The Legal Status of the Slave in South Carolina, 1670–1740," *The Journal of Southern History* 28, no. 4 (1962): 471, https://doi.org/10.2307/2205410.

43 Wood, 153, 154.

44 Middleton and Lombard, *Colonial America*, 222.

45 Adele Hast, "The Legal Status of the Negro in Virginia 1705–1765," *The Journal of Negro History* 54, no. 3 (1969): 217, https://doi.org/10.2307/2716667.

46 Wilbert E. Moore, "Slave Law and the Social Structure," *The Journal of Negro History* 26, no. 2 (1941): 174, https://doi.org/10.2307/2715249.
47 Hast, "The Legal Status of the Negro in Virginia," 232.
48 Coombs, "The Phases of Conversion," 334.
49 Hast, 232.
50 Hast, 218.
51 Mary Newton Standard, *Colonial Virginia Its People and Customs* (Philadelphia: J. B. Lippincott Company, 1917), 126, 142–43, Google Books.
52 Wilma King, *African American Childhoods: Historical Perspectives from Slavery to Civil Rights* (New York: Palgrave Macmillan, 2005), 12.
53 King, *African American Childhoods*, 12, 16–18.
54 C. Dallett Hemphill, "Sibling Relations in Early American Childhoods: A Cross-Cultural Analysis," in *Children in Colonial Times*, ed. James Marten (New York: New York University Press, 2007), 84.
55 G. E. Thomas, "Puritans, Indians, and the Concept of Race," *The New England Quarterly* 48, no. 1 (1975): 8, https://doi.org/10.2307/364910.
56 Newell, 192.
57 John A. Sainsbury, "Indian Labor in Early Rhode Island," *The New England Quarterly* 48, no. 3 (1975): 379, https://doi.org/10.2307/364865.
58 Newell, 208.
59 Shane White, "Slavery in the North," *OAH Magazine of History* 17, no. 3 (2003): 18, www.jstor.org/stable/25163595.
60 David Roediger and Martin H. Blatt, eds., *The Meaning of Slavery in the North* (New York: Garland Publishing, Inc., 1998), 8, 11.
61 Jared Ross Hardesty, *Black Lives, Native Lands, White Worlds: A History of Slavery in New England* (Boston, MA: Bright Leaf, 2019), 48.
62 Hardesty, *Black Lives, Native Lands, White Worlds*, 31.
63 Hardesty, 29.
64 Newell, 210.
65 Hardesty, 76.
66 Anne Farrow, Joel Lang, and Jennifer Frank, *Complicity: How the North Promoted, Prolonged, and Profited from Slavery* (New York: Ballentine Books, 2005), 51.
67 White, "Slavery in the North," 18.
68 Hardesty, 75.
69 Roediger and Blatt, *Slavery in the North*, 10.
70 Hardesty, 88–91.
71 Hardesty, 88–91.
72 Beckert, 36.
73 Beckert, 45–46.
74 Virginia Postrel, *The Fabric of Civilization: How Textiles Made the World* (New York: Basic Books, 2020), 130.
75 Beckert, 49.
76 Alice Morse Earle, *Costume of Colonial Times* (New York: Charles Scribner's Sons, 1894), 83; Florence M. Montgomery, *Textiles in America 1650–1870* (New York: W. W. Norton & Company, 2007), 199.
77 Joseph E. Inikori and Stanley L. Engerman, eds., *The Atlantic Slave Trade: Effects on Economies, Societies and Peoples in Africa, the Americas, and Europe* (Duke University Press, 1992), 157, 169–70, https://doi.org/10.2307/j.ctv1220pd1. Ronald Bailey, "The Other Side of Slavery: Black Labor, Cotton, and Textile Industrialization in Great Britain and the United States," *Agricultural History* 68, no. 2 (1994): 43, www.jstor.org/stable/3744401.
78 Earle, *Costume of Colonial Times*, 83.
79 Loranger and Sanders, 686.
80 Elise Niles, *A Narrative of the Life and Adventures of Venture, a Native of Africa: But Resident above Sixty Years in the United States of America* (New London: C. Holt, 1798), 1–13; W. Shirley, *A Narrative of the Most Remarkable Particulars in the Life of James Albert Ukawsaw Gronniosaw, an African Prince, as Related by Himself* (Bath: W. Gye, 1770), 1–13.
81 Niles, *Narrative of the Life and Adventures of Venture*, 1–13.
82 Shirley, *The Life of James Albert Ukawsaw Gronniosaw*, 1–13.
83 Susan M. Ouellette, *Us Textile Production in Historical Perspective: A Case Study from Massachusetts* (New York: Routledge; Taylor and Francis Group, 2012), 31.
84 William R. Bagnall, *The Textile Industries of the United States*, vol. 1 (Cambridge: Riverside Press, 1893), 13, 15, Google Books.
85 Staples and Shaw, *Clothing Through American History*, 153.
86 Rolla Milton Tryon, *Household Manufactures in the United States 1640–1860: A Study in Industrial History* (Chicago: The University of Chicago Press, 1917), 49.
87 Standard, *Colonial Virginia*, 55.
88 Tryon, *Household Manufactures*, 26.
89 Ruth Wallis Herndon and John E. Murray, eds., *Children Bound to Labor: The Pauper Apprentice System in Early America* (Ithaca: Cornell University Press, 2009), 206.
90 Abbott, "A Study of the Early History of Child Labor in America," 21.
91 George Francis Dow, *Every Day Life in the Massachusetts Bay Colony* (New York: Dover Publications, 1988), 135.

92 Laurel Thatcher Ulrich, *The Age of Homespun: Objects and Stories in the Creation of an American Myth* (New York: Vintage Books, 2001), 157.
93 Bagnall, *The Textile Industries of the United States*, 37, 48.
94 Mark A. Turdo, "May Love Set You to Spinning: A Sketch of 18th-Century Moravian Textile Production in Bethlehem and Nazareth, Pennsylvania," *Transactions of the Moravian Historical Society* 31 (2000): 67–68, www.jstor.org/stable/41179484.
95 Bagnall, 26.
96 Ben Marsh, "Silk Hopes in Colonial South Carolina," *The Journal of Southern History* 78, no. 4 (2012): 813, 821, www.jstor.org/stable/23795645.
97 Marsh, "Silk Hopes in Colonial South Carolina," 813, 821.
98 Marsh, 813, 821.
99 Earle, 102.
100 Ouellette, *Us Textile Production in Historical Perspective*, 86.
101 Bagnall, 26.
102 Staples and Shaw, 153.
103 Standard, 196–98.
104 Fischer, *Albion's Seed*, 358.
105 Fischer, 358.
106 Standard, 196–97.
107 Earle, 75.
108 Fischer, 358.
109 Eulanda A. Sanders, "The Politics of Textiles Used in African American Slave Clothing," *Textile Society of America Symposium Proceedings*, October 2012, 1, Digital Commons@ University of Nebraska-Lincon.
110 Sanders, "The Politics of Textiles," 1.
111 Dow, *Every Day Life in the Massachusetts Bay Colony*, 94.
112 Max Hamrick, *Organic Fiber Dyeing: The Colonial Williamsburg Method* (Paducah: American Quilter's Society, 2013), 11.
113 Hamrick, *Organic Fiber Dyeing*, 90.
114 Josephine Paterek, *Encyclopedia of American Indian Costume* (New York: W. W. Norton & Company, 1994), 445.
115 Cecil Lubell, ed., *Textile Collections of the World: Volume 1 United States and Canada* (New York: Van Nostrand Reinhold Company, 1976), 131; Hamrick, 90.
116 Hamrick, 89.
117 Peter M. Molloy, *Homespun to Factory Made: Woolen Textiles in America* (North Andover: Merrimack Valley Textile Museum, 1977), 42.
118 Dow, 95.
119 Dow, 95.
120 Lubell, *Textile Collections of the World: Volume 1 United States and Canada*, 131; Hamrick, 90.
121 Mary Schoeser and Celia Rufey, *English and American Textiles: From 1790 to the Present* (New York: Thames and Hudson, 1989), 41–42.
122 Staples and Shaw, 176.
123 *Boston Gazette*, April 18–25, 1720; *Boston Gazette*, June 16–23, 1735.
124 Schoeser and Rufey, *English and American Textiles*, 41–42.
125 Staples and Shaw, 176.
126 Hamrick, 14.
127 R. C. Nash, "South Carolina Indigo, European Textiles, and the British Atlantic Economy in the Eighteenth Century," *The Economic History Review* 63, no. 2 (2010): 363, www.jstor.org/stable/27771617.
128 Nash, "South Carolina Indigo," 363.
129 Elise Pinckney, ed., *The Letterbook of Eliza Lucas Pinckney 1739–1762* (Columbia: The University of South Carolina Press, 1972), ix–xx.
130 Pinckeny, *The Letterbook of Eliza Lucas Pinckney*, ix–xx.
131 G. Terry Sharrer, "Indigo in Carolina, 1671–1796," *The South Carolina Historical Magazine* 72, no. 2 (1971): 95–97, www.jstor.org/stable/27567037.
132 *Boston Gazette*, May 7, 1759.
133 Kathleen J. Bragdon, *Native People of Southern New England 1650–1775* (Norman: University of Oklahoma Press, 2009), 136.
134 Bragdon, *Native People*, 136.
135 Paterek, *Encyclopedia of American Indian Costume*, 450.
136 William Hugh Grove, Gregory A. Stiverson, and Patrick H. Butler, "Virginia in 1732: The Travel Journal of William Hugh Grove," *The Virginia Magazine of History and Biography* 85, no. 1 (January 1977): 30.
137 Bragdon, 134.
138 Bragdon, 157.
139 Turdo, "May Love Set You to Spinning," 68.
140 E. Merton Coulter, "When John Wesley Preached in Georgia," *The Georgia Historical Quarterly* 9, no. 4 (1925): 330–33, www.jstor.org/stable/40575832.
141 Gallay, 303.
142 *Boston Newsletter*, October 4, 1739.
143 Grove, Stiverson, and Butler, "Virginia in 1732," 31.
144 Loranger and Sanders, 685.
145 Loranger and Sanders, 692.
146 John Woolman, *The Journal of John Woolman* (Boston: Houghton Mifflin Company, 1909), 109, Google Books; John Woolman, *The Works of John Woolman in Two Parts*

(Philadelphia: Benjamin & Thomas Kite, 1818), 209, 264, Google Books.

147 Barbara M. Starke, Lillian O. Holloman, and Barbara K. Nordquist, eds., *African American Dress and Adornment: A Cultural Perspective* (Dubuque: Kendall Hunt Publishing Company, 1990), 82–92.

148 Andrea Feeser, *Red, White & Black Make Blue: Indigo in the Fabric of Colonial South Carolina Life* (Athens: The University of Georgia Press, 2013), 32.

149 Spencer R. Crew, Lonnie G. Bunch III, and Clement A. Price, eds., *Memories of the Enslaved: Voices from the Slave Narratives* (Santa Barbara: Praeger, 2015), 41, 65.

150 Crew, Bunch, and Price, *Memories of the Enslaved*, 41, 65.

151 Fischer, 389.

152 Grove, Stiverson, and Butler, 32.

153 Standard, 115, 177.

154 Susan Borrows Swan, *Plain and Fancy: American Women and Their Needlework, 1700–1850* (New York: Routledge, 1977), 36.

155 Crew, Bunch, and Price, 43, 52, 63.

156 Crew, Bunch, and Price, 43, 52, 63.

157 Crew, Bunch, and Price, 43, 52, 63.

158 Feeser, *Red, White & Black Make Blue*, 32.

159 Fischer, 359.

160 Standard, 204.

161 Staples and Shaw, 127.

162 Hamrick, 13; Staples and Shaw, 127.

163 Feeser, 25.

164 Staples and Shaw, 127.

165 Standard, 205.

166 Fischer, 359.

167 Fischer, 358.

168 Estelle Ansley Worrell, *Children's Costume in America 1607–1910* (New York: Charles Scribner's Sons, 1980), 24.

169 Alice Morse Earle, *Two Centuries of Costume in America 1620–1820*, vol. 1, 2nd ed. (Williamstown: Corner House Publishers, 1974), 88.

170 Edward Warwick, Henry C. Pitz, and Alexander Wyckoff, *Early American Dress: The Colonial and Revolutionary Periods* (New York: Bonanza Books, 1965), 239.

171 Karen Calvert, *Children in the House: The Material Culture of Early Childhood 1600–1900* (Boston: Northeastern University Press, 1992), 79, 92.

172 Warwick, Pitz, and Wyckoff, *Early American Dress*, 249.

173 Bagnall, 14.

174 Ouellette, 86.

175 Bagnall, 14.

176 Calvert, *Children in the House*, 44.

177 Warwick, Pitz, and Wyckoff, 239.

178 Warwick, Pitz, and Wyckoff, 257.

179 Calvert, 44.

180 Standard, 198.

181 Worrell, *Children's Costume in America*, 24.

CHAPTER FOUR

1760–1800

Leading up to the Revolutionary War, colonial America was 13 colonies strong, with several economically thriving communities and a growing population. Philadelphia was the largest city, with a population of 23,000, New York recorded 18,000, Boston 16,000, Charles Town 8,000, and Newport 7,500. Salem and Marblehead, Massachusetts, reported 3,000 residents, as did Baltimore, Norfolk, and Savannah in the southern colonies. In addition to the population growth in the colonies' established cities, the countryside was expanding with settlers even faster. Virginia and North Carolina were experiencing population growth in the Piedmont region located between the Appalachian Mountains and the Atlantic coast.[1] With this increase in population, there was naturally a rise in the number of children in each established colony. While children from families of wealth often flourished, children of lower income struggled, as did their parents. As Indigenous and African slavery continued in the colonies, the population of mixed-race and slave children continued to grow. The solidifying social structure, as well as the legal system, continued to dictate the role each of these children was assigned for their lifetime.[2]

Events leading up to the American Revolution intensified the push to create homespun textiles and clothing as a form of resistance against the British government.[3] Once the Revolution was over, the newly formed United States needed to find a way to develop its own textile industry. No one in the new republic had the textile production knowledge to incorporate all the technological advances used in Britain. That would change with the immigration of Samuel Slater and the development of the first textile mill in Rhode Island.[4] In this newly created textile industry, enslaved children in the South cultivated cotton that poor children in the North prepared and spun for cloth production.[5] Clothing styles for colonial children simplified leading up to and after the American Revolution. Boys transitioned more quickly to adult-inspired clothing pieces, while dresses for girls became less complex in design.[6] As servants in wealthy or middle-class households, Indigenous children were given simple garments to wear, while enslaved plantation children were often not given enough clothing to fully cover their bodies.[7]

COMMUNITIES: SOCIAL AND POLITICAL STRUCTURE

SOUTHERN COMMUNITIES

Eighteenth-century planter and merchant parents put their children to work in family businesses at

DOI: 10.4324/9781003230441-5

an early age, managing plantations, trade transactions, and slaves. Carolina colonists placed emphasis on productive work for all members of the household. Parents were committed to building strong economic foundations for their children and equipping their offspring with the means to continue to build the family fortune.[8] Boys were prepared to take over executive roles as adults, while girls were prepared for managerial positions, especially on plantations. Girls often supervised a dairy, kitchen garden, or the education of younger siblings as part of their training. As more African slaves entered the region, there was less English or European-educated labor to assist planters and merchants. To address this decrease in educated assistance, women and children within elite southern family circles were placed in secretarial and managerial positions.[9]

A goal in the socialization of children was to prepare them to take their proper place in a hierarchical culture. All children in Virginia, regardless of social class, were taught the regional formal rights of conduct from a book entitled, *The School of Manners*.[10] Children ofVirginia were required to learn these rules by rote as a way to discipline their will. The higher the child's status in society, the more rigid the cultural rules.[11] In regard to formal schooling, the Virginia Upper-class felt that learning was imperative for their children, but among the general public, education brought dissension and disobedience in the hierarchal social structure. The well-to-do hired private tutors for their own children and sponsored schools for families with wealth and position. There were no efforts to educate the lower classes in Virginia. It is no surprise that slaves were

Figure 4.1 Fenwick Hall Plantation located on John's Island, Charleston, South Carolina. Initial construction took place in 1730. (Frances Benjamin, *Fenwick Hall Plantation, John's Island, Charleston County, South Carolina*, 1938, photograph, Library of Congress.)

Figure 4.2 The Charleston Orphan House, South Carolina, founded in 1790. (*The Orphan House-Charleston, S.C.*, photograph, Library of Congress.)

forbidden to read and write. If a slave was caught reading or writing, they were punished by having a finger amputated.[12]

Anglo-European Poor Children

In colonial America, children born to poor or unmarried parents were a challenge for officials. Before the Revolution, town officials were often seen as the parents of a child who could not be provided for in the community. Poor, orphan, and illegitimate children were taken by the courts from their parents or parent and bound out to a pauper apprenticeship.[13] Illegitimate children by law were placed under the umbrella of county magistrates who chose which boys and girls to bind out.[14] A substantial number of bound out children came from homes with a single woman as the head of the household.[15] In this system, girls were bound until they were 18 and boys until they were 21.[16] Binding out poor and illegitimate children in Virginia and North Carolina served as a way of controlling child labor in the community, as well as a welfare policy.[17]

In contrast to Virginia, South Carolina's system for overseeing the poor in the 18th century was handled exclusively through Anglican vestries.[18] In the best situation, poor children were taken care of by a relative in the parish. If a child was orphaned, with no relations, they were bound out to pauper apprenticeships until they reached maturity.[19] Charleston, South Carolina, due to the size of the city, established a Poor House within its boundaries. The Poor House was part hospital, part insane asylum, and part homeless shelter for those who could not care for themselves. Children too young to leave their mothers resided in the Poor House. Children between the ages of nine and 12 attended a charity boarding school, while older children were bound out to masters in pauper apprenticeships. Charleston city officials also saw the need for the creation of an Orphan House in 1790 to keep children with no family ties from residing in the Poor House.[20]

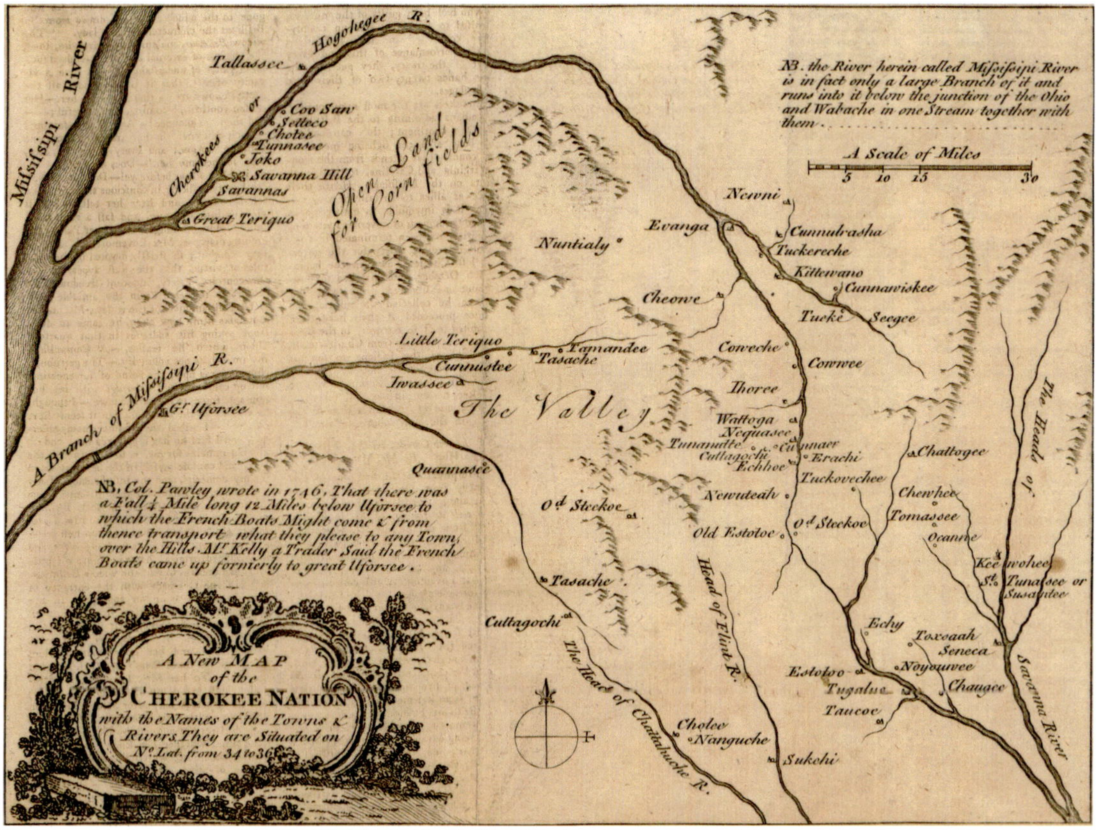

Figure 4.3 (Thomas Kitchin, cartographer, *A new map of the Cherokee Nation: with the names of the towns & rivers: they are situated on No. lat. from 34 to 36*, 1760, 17 x 23 cm in *London Magazine* (London: 1760), Library of Congress.)

Indigenous Children

In addition to the struggles poor children faced in their communities, Indigenous children were often caught in the middle of violent conflicts. Relations between the Indigenous nations and the southern colonies were full of complexities leading up to the American Revolution, which adversely affected children in both communities. Beginning in the early 1760s, Cherokee towns were attacked by settler military groups to scare the Cherokee into submission. Instead of submitting to the British Crown, the Cherokee Nation retaliated. Several Carolina settler communities were destroyed in the process.[21] The South Carolina leader of the settler militia, William Henry Dayton, ordered that every Indigenous town be burned, and every captured Indigenous person enslaved. Those enslaved became the property of the taker. In addition to the destruction of the Cherokee communities, the land inhabited by the Cherokee people became the property of the new republic.[22] Destruction of Indigenous towns and the families who lived within these communities continued into the 1780s.[23]

The Cherokee were not the only Indigenous people fighting for the right to remain on the lands they inhabited. Massive sections of land were taken from Indigenous populations throughout the southern United States.[24] In what became known as the Yazoo Land Fraud of 1795, 35 million Indigenous acres were sold for $500,000 by Georgia Governor George Mathews and the Georgia Assembly.[25] The acres sold were located along the Tennessee River in the region of future northern Alabama, and along the Mississippi River from south of modern-day Memphis to future Vicksburg, Mississippi.[26] As in most land sales in early America, the Georgia state government was selling Indigenous land that was not theirs to sell. The Cherokee, Creek, Chickasaw, and Choctaw people had sovereignty over the millions of acres sold. With the large-scale dispossession of land and depopulation, Indigenous nations within English colonial territory in the South either became extinct or migrated westward. The Indigenous slave trade, widespread disease, and land loss wiped out dozens of Indigenous tribes. With this mass depopulation of Indigenous people, the Indigenous slave trade came to an end in the late 18th century.[27]

African Children

The practice of taking Indigenous land expanded the plantation system to the lower Mississippi Valley. Slave-holding farms and plantations were also developed along the Missouri and Ohio rivers. Just as in the southern colonies, African slavery became key to the economic, social, and political lives of settlers in these newly established areas.[28] As African slavery continued in Virginia, Delaware, Maryland, and North and South Carolina, it was firmly established in Georgia. Initially, enslaved men, women, and children in Georgia were imported from the West Indies and South Carolina. With the need for more slave labor on Georgia plantations, shipments began to arrive directly from Africa in 1766.[29] Between the years 1767 and 1774, the Savannah-based company of Cowper and Telfairs imported 11 shiploads of enslaved men, women, and children.[30] At the signing of the Declaration of Independence, an estimated 500,000 slaves were held by slaveholders in all 13 colonies. The highest concentration of enslaved men, women, and children existed in Maryland, Delaware, Virginia, North Carolina, South Carolina, and Georgia.[31]

During the American Revolution, planters began experimenting with growing large crops of

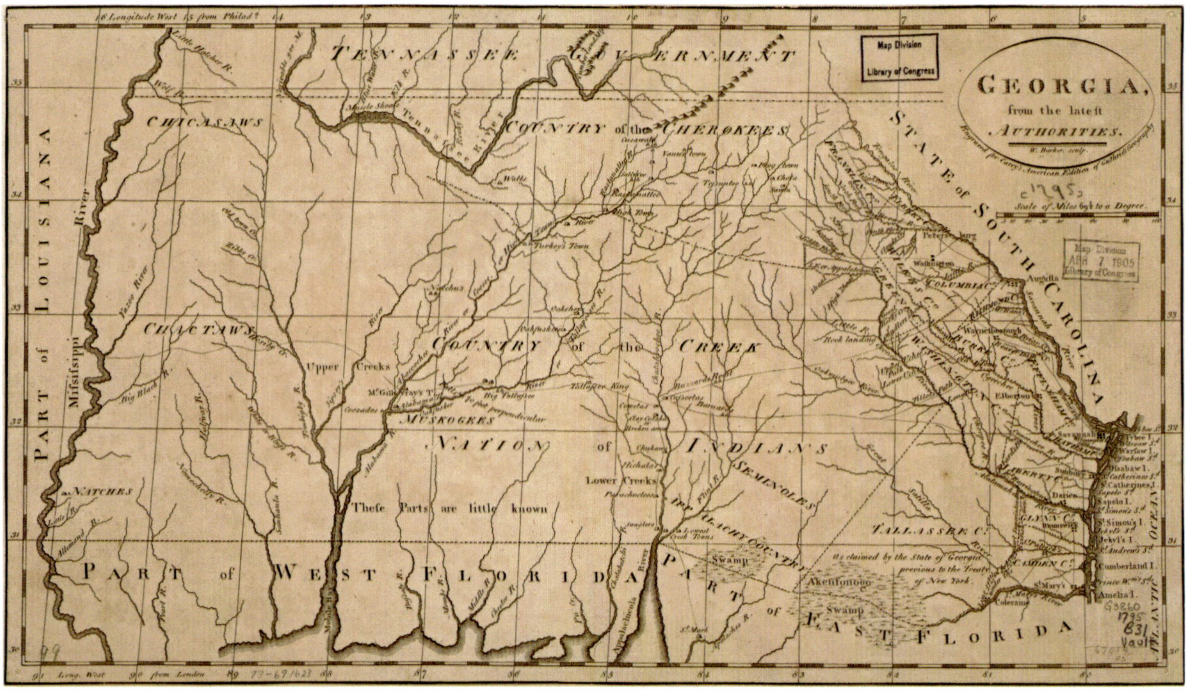

Figure 4.4 Map detailing the location of the Indigenous nations in Georgia and Southern Tennessee in 1795. (W. Barker, Matthew Carey, and William Guthrie, cartographers, *Georgia, from the Latest Authorities*, 1795, 23 X 40 cm, Library of Congress.)

Figure 4.5 (N. Currier, *Declaration of Independence: July 4th 1776*, 1835, hand-colored lithograph, New York, Library of Congress.)

cotton due to the nonexistent textile trade with Britain.[32] This rise in cotton production coincided with an increase in enslaved children. More children were taken from their homes in Africa, transported to the colonies, and sold into slavery. In the cargo hold of a ship, a child under four feet four inches took up less space than a full-sized adult. Five smaller children could fit in the same space as four adults. This meant more profit for slave traders and a longer period of enslavement for the master who bought them.[33] Historians have estimated that 34 percent of the slaves traded during the height of the slave trade were children.[34] Early Caribbean planters who migrated to the colonies understood the worth and value of enslaved children. In Barbados, these plantation owners learned the method of breeding children to create their own slave population. These large numbers of enslaved children could be used for labor when they reached working age or traded for profit. Adult male slaves on Barbados plantations were encouraged to have three to four wives, which could lead to as many as 30 children born into slavery. The cost of bringing up enslaved children was minimal, while the labor and trade of a child were profitable.[35]

In a plantation system, children too young to work often spent their days in a nursery organized by the mistress of the plantation and supervised by older enslaved women. Other plantations left children completely on their own during the day while their parents worked.[36] Slaveholders did not see the need to nurture children, only to provide for their basic needs to ensure they grew to become adult workers. To prepare them for a lifetime of labor, slave masters trained young enslaved children to gather wood, clean houses, wash clothes, spin fibers, weave cloth, make clothing, carry water to field hands, assist in food preparation, hoe in rice, tobacco, and cotton fields, and eventually take over the jobs of the enslaved adults.[37] By the age of

Figure 4.6 Male and female slaves at Fort Kachao. (John Georg Purmann, *Schwarze von Kachao und Bissao, welche manioc bereiten*, 1778, engraving, 16.2 X 13.4 cm (6.3 x 5.2 in). Courtesy of the John Carter Brown Library.)

12 to 14, enslaved children were expected to work like adults either out in the fields or in the plantation house. Some children were treated well, like Henry Rogers, who shared fond memories in his slave narrative about his time as an enslaved child in Georgia among 15 to 20 other enslaved men, women, and children.[38] In stark contrast were the experiences of George Womble. George recalled waiting tables, house cleaning, and taking care of his master's three children as a young boy. He also vividly remembered the physical beatings and emotional abuse he endured at the hands of his master.[39]

NORTHERN COMMUNITIES

In the 1765 Boston census, 52 percent of the British and European population were children under 16.[40] Free education was provided for boys in neighborhood schools. Boys not attending school were already working as apprentices in shops, on ships, on farms, or for mercantile counting houses. Boys who attended school graduated at the age of 14 and began to work as adults in the community. New England boys were expected to take on the role of an adult male early in life in work and in war.[41] In contrast to the education of boys in New England, free public schooling was not available to female children. Girls could take lessons in handwriting, crafts, dancing, and other artistic skills from a private tutor. Most often, girls prepared for adult life by doing domestic chores in the home.[42] If schooling was offered to Anglo-European girls, it was often in the form of a 'dame' school. These schools often took place in neighborhoods where a woman in the community, for a fee, gave lessons on elementary reading, and math in her home. The focus of neighborhood schools for girls was often

Figure 4.7 Photograph of a slave nursery at Eliot's Plantation. (Henry P. Moore, *Nursery at Elliot's Plantation, Hilton Head, S.C., South Carolina Hilton Head Island*, 1862, photograph, Library of Congress.)

practicing plain sewing and knitting skills. These were seen as essential skills girls needed to make and mend clothing as well as properly provide other textile needs in their homes as adults.[43]

In the mid-18th century, the Moravians created one of the earliest boarding schools for girls in Bethlehem, Pennsylvania.[44] Before the establishment of the boarding school, the Moravians were known throughout the colonies for the fine textiles they created in their community. The Moravians provided a well-rounded education for girls of wealthy families similar to a boy's education. In addition, girls were taught intensive needlework techniques. In New England, needlework classes ranged from fine silk embroidery to tent stitches on canvas. Girls from Upper-class families, who could afford to send their children to intensive training schools, were taught more complicated needlework skills. Several of the stitches taught at the more expensive schools included canvas work, crewelwork, lace work, and tambour. The more elaborate stitches could be used later in life to adorn the clothing and furnishings of a prosperous home where servants or enslaved individuals could tend to daily chores, leaving the decorative work to the wife and daughters of the household.[45]

Anglo-European Poor Children

It was often the elite class that took in poor children to assist them in the day-to-day responsibilities of running a large household. While wealthy families networked together to protect their families and their economic status, the poor had no connections to others who could assist them. Illegitimate, abandoned, orphaned, or destitute children had to rely on a parent or city officials to bind them out in

Figure 4.8 Embroidery sampler completed by 13-year-old Isabel Newby in 1742. (Isabel Newby, *Embroidered Sampler*, 1742, silk thread on linen, 12 x 8 ¾ in (30.5 X 22.2 cm), gift of Miriam Troop-Zuger, 2000. Courtesy of the Metropolitan Museum of Art.)

Figure 4.9 This embroidered coverlet was originally bed curtains and three bed valences created by teenager Mary Breed in 1770 of New London County, Connecticut. (Mary Breed, *Embroidered Coverlet*, 1742, linen and cotton fabric with wool embroidery, 90 ¾ X 89 in (230.5 X 226.1 cm), Rogers Fund, 1922. Courtesy of the Metropolitan Museum of Art.)

Figure 4.10 Moravian boarding school for girls established in the 18th century. The Moravian Sisters' House is located on the right side of the school. (Historic American Buildings Survey, *Bell House, 56 West Church Street, Bethlehem, Northampton County, PA., Pennsylvania Northampton County Bethlehem*, 1933, photograph, Library of Congress.)

service or apprenticeships.[46] In Connecticut, Massachusetts, and Rhode Island, magistrates and masters worked together to bind at-risk children into pauper apprenticeships. These children were placed in community homes meant to instruct them in the skills needed to take their proper position in society.[47] Statistically, boys were bound out in higher numbers than girls and for longer periods of time. Boys also received more education, skill training, and freedom dues at the end of their apprenticeships. In Massachusetts, boys were trained in a trade needed in the community, in husbandry by local farmers, or in some cases as a gentleman. Girls were trained at first to spin fibers and then transitioned into learning housewifery skills. A majority of the male pauper apprentices were given freedom dues at the end of their indenture which consisted of two freedom suits and financial assistance. Female pauper apprentices were not given freedom dues or clothing at the end of their term. The young women either continued as servants in their masters' households or married.[48]

In Boston, specifically, many of the children who were bound to pauper apprenticeships were orphaned or abandoned in the city's almshouse for the poor. Between 1740 and 1763, Boston experienced a devastating military campaign, a smallpox epidemic, and the Seven Years' War between the British and the French. This placed Boston in an economic depression with thousands of poor women and children in the community by the early 1760s. City officials were focused on assisting boys by finding ways to secure a better future for them in Boston's uncertain economy.[49] In New

England, the number of pauper apprenticeships coincided with periods of time when local farmers, artisans, and households were financially stable. This allowed prospective masters the necessary funding to take in pauper apprentices. Connecticut, Massachusetts, and Rhode Island all experienced an increase in binding out poor children soon after the American Revolution as the economy became more stable.[50]

Indigenous Children

In addition to the elite and poor children, there were hundreds of Indigenous children in Boston in 1765, however little is known of their experiences.[51] What has been recorded links Indigenous children to indentured servitude and pauper apprenticeships in New England. At first, pauper apprenticeships were primarily organized for British and European children in the colonies. As time went on Indigenous children, considered tied to a regional tribe of New England, were also bound out by community officials. Poverty-stricken Indigenous children were often bound out as domestic servants or farm laborers The process of binding out Indigenous children was similar to binding out British and European children. Assigned local officials known as selectmen chose the children they felt needed to be bound out of their impoverished Indigenous homes. Indenturing and binding out poor Indigenous children continued until the mid-19th century.[52]

While Indigenous children were bound out in New England, other Indigenous children in regions surrounding the area were innocent victims of land wars. During the last quarter of the 18th century, Indigenous dispossession of land was taking place on a massive scale. The region most affected by this surge was located to the west

Figure 4.11 A Lenape (Delaware) man and woman with their child. (Thomas Campanius Holm, *Om the Americaners urt och Bestaffenhet wid Virginien och Nya Swerige*, 1654, engraving, 15.4 x 12.2 cm (6 x 4.8 in). Courtesy of the John Carter Brown Library.)

of the Appalachian Mountains and east of the Mississippi River. The Delaware, Shawnee, and other Algonquian people by the Ohio River, the Iroquois Confederacy near Lake Ontario, and the Abenaki in the Northeast, were all facing constant invasion. Thousands of settlers poured into their lands, erecting small log homes, while clearing and tilling the land. This substantial movement of settlers driving deeper into Native land rose during the American Revolution and surged higher after the war. In the state of New York alone, over three million acres of land were taken from the Iroquois.[53] Indigenous villages were burned and looted, leaving the Indigenous people homeless with no means to support themselves.[54]

African Children

As the African slave trade flourished in the 1760s, abolitionists in New England began speaking out against the horrific practice of slavery. Slavery in the northern colonies had expanded to include an estimated 47,000 men, women, and children.[55] Rhode Island was still the largest slave trading colony during the Revolution and continued to expand its trade into the early 19th century. It was also home to one of the earliest abolitionist movements.[56] While many powerful Rhode Island families were heavily involved in the slave trade, Rhode Island state legislature began establishing laws to slowly abolish the slave trade in 1779.[57] In both Rhode Island and Connecticut, gradual emancipation laws, created to phase out slavery, went into effect in 1784. Rather than end slavery abruptly by taking away all of a master's slaves at once, children born after March 1, 1784, were freed once they reached adulthood.[58] In contrast, the Supreme Judicial Court of Massachusetts ordered in 1783 that no citizen had the right to hold human property. All slaves in Massachusetts were immediately set free.[59]

Emancipation changed the structure of pauper apprenticeship. Children born to free Black parents in New England could be bound to a pauper apprenticeship if community officials deemed it necessary. Binding out children of free parents of color became increasingly common, especially in communities with a large Black population.[60] Differences existed in what skills Black children were trained in during their pauper apprenticeships. Instead of learning a trade, most young boys from the Black community were funneled into household service positions. In addition, freedom dues or suits were often omitted at the end of their indenture.[61] As pauper apprenticeships diminished for British and European children, they increased for Indigenous and Black children.[62] Of the New England states, Rhode Island in particular bound out a significant number of Indigenous, Black, mustee, and mulatto children in 1790. Before the American Revolution, Rhode Island made a clear distinction in documentation between the Indigenous population and the African population in the region. After the American Revolution, racial mixing in community records became prevalent.[63],[64] Instead of clearly distinguishing Indigenous people from mixed-race or African people, New England documentation began grouping Indigenous individuals together with Black and mixed-race community members.[65]

As time progressed, slave labor and pauper apprenticeships began to drop in the late 18th century as textile mills began to take shape in New England. Child labor was moving out of the household, farm, and workshop into textile manufacturing. Mill owners and supervisors became the new masters of children whose labor paved the way for the ultimate success of the 19th-century textile industry.[66] From the beginning of colonization, the work of children was utilized as a community and economic asset to move the nation forward.[67] As America neared an industrial revolution of its own, the combined labor of children in the northern states and enslaved children in the southern states became the driving force behind the success of the first attempt to produce textiles on a large scale in the newly formed United States.

TEXTILES AND TEXTILE PRODUCTION

TEXTILE PRODUCTION BEFORE THE AMERICAN REVOLUTION

In the mid-18th century, homespun activity in the colonies grew as settler communities expanded on Indigenous land. Beginning in the early 1760s, Parliament imposed large taxes on imported goods on British ships, which included textiles. British taxes were attached to the importation of silk, cloth mixed with silk, calicos, cambric, and French lightweight cottons. In resistance to these heavy taxes, cloth production increased in colonial homes and communities.[68] In 1764, several textile manufacturing houses developed throughout the northern colonies to help offset the costs of taxed textiles. In Philadelphia, an association was created for the manufacturing of linen. After the buildings were erected, over 100 adults and children were employed to spin and weave coarse linen for the public. On Long Island in the same year, a group of gentlemen established a woolen manufacturing company that advertised the making of fine broadcloth in a variety of colors. They employed wool combers, weavers, clothiers, shearers, dyers, spinners, and carders.[69] In the city of New York, 'The Society for the Promotion of Arts, Agriculture, and Economy' organized a linen manufacturing system under the direction of Obadiah Wells to employ individuals who needed work, while also providing less expensive textiles to the community. The factory hired spinners to prepare yarn for weaving, and sold colonial-made cloth.[70] All of these textile production efforts provided local cloth options to colonial families.

As more taxes were attached to items imported on British ships with the Townshend Duties Act, colonial city officials and community members in

Figure 4.12 Loom factory and calico print shop located in Comly Ville, a suburb of Philadelphia. (William L. Briton, *Comlyville Near Frankford, Philadelphia*, 1830, lithograph, *L.A. Godey & Company*, 1830, Library of Congress.)

1767 took steps to further encourage the production of textiles and other goods in the colonies. Boston, Providence and Newport, Rhode Island, as well as Windam, Connecticut, were the first cities to take active steps to promote community-wide textile production.[71] The push to create textiles as a form of resistance to the British government spread throughout the northern colonies. Manufacturing houses were recorded to spring up throughout the region. Outside of the manufacturing houses, private homes throughout the colony were producing woolen and linen textiles. According to New York's Governor Moore, in 1767, almost every home with children in the region was involved in producing textiles for their families. While the adult family members oversaw the management of creating textiles, their children were instructed to card and spin fibers in preparation for weaving.[72]

Patriotic campaigns against taxed imports encouraged females of all ages to spin yarn for the production of colonial cloth. In response, females of all ages and social classes began spinning yarn across New England. In March, 1766, a group of 18 daughters from wealthy families in Providence, Rhode Island, established the 'Daughters of Liberty.'[73] The purpose of the organization was to spin fibers into yarn from sunrise to sunset in support of their community. Spinning meetings similar to the 'Daughters of Liberty' organization began to spread. Between March, 1768 and October, 1770, 60 spinning meetings were reported throughout New England. Most meetings took place in the home of ministers where young girls and women could gather to create yarn for the support of the minister's family or those in need of textiles in the community.[74] In Ipswich on June 22, 1769, 77 women and young girls gathered at the home of Reverend John Cleveland with their spinning wheels. By six o'clock that evening, the group had spun 400 yards of linen, 700 yards of cotton, and 600 yards of tow.[75] Public spinning demonstrations also sprung up in New England communities. Spinning demonstrations brought together men, women, and children in the community as they all participated in spinning yarn for cloth production.[76] According to newspaper articles from Boston, Braintree, and Ipswich, Massachusetts, as well as Providence, and Newport, Rhode Island, children from the ages of seven to 11 participated in spinning bees hosted by members of the community.[77]

The development of manufacturing companies continued as the colonies neared the American Revolution. The Manufacturing House in Boston closed in the mid-18th century but was reopened under the supervision of John Brown and William Molineux in 1770. Brown and Molinex were both given sections of the house to care for as well as to produce cloth. John Brown supervised the production of cotton and linen cloth in his section of the manufacturing house, while Molineux concentrated on the production of worsted wool.[78] In addition to producing fabric as a sign of resistance, dyeing cloth also became a patriotic endeavor. Newly established textile manufacturing mills in Virginia took pride in the shades of color they could produce. The Nomini Fulling Mill, built on the Nomini River, was outfitted for fulling, dressing, shearing, and dyeing. In the *Virginia Gazette* of 1770, the operator of the mill, Benjamin Brooks, promised high-quality dye work in any colors on jean fabric, fustian, wools, and cottons.[79] In 1772, the immigration of English fabric printer John Hewson to Philadelphia provided a way for colonists to buy high-quality, locally printed fabrics without having to rely on British imports. John Hewson was a master printer with years of experience bleaching, dyeing, as well as block printing linen, cotton, and calico in a variety of images and colors.[80] Through the work of John Hewson and other skilled textile artists, Philadelphia became a leader in early American cloth production.

Philadelphia's role in expanding colonial textile production solidified in 1775. The United Company of Philadelphia for Promoting American

Figure 4.13 Hand-printed cotton quilt center created by John Hewson. (John Hewson, *Quilt Center*, 1790, printed cotton, 27 5/8 x 29 1/2 in (70.2 x 74.9 cm), gift of David S. and Elizabeth W. Quackenbush, 2005. Courtesy of the Metropolitan Museum of Art.)

Manufactures was established to create woolen, cotton, and linen for public consumption.[81] The organization purchased a house on the corner of Ninth and Market Street, which became the location of textile manufacturing until 1778 when the British Army overtook and evacuated Philadelphia. Before the British Army invaded Philadelphia, the American Manufactory purchased a newly invented spinning machine developed by Christopher Tully to speed up the manufacturing process of woven textiles. This is the first reference to the invention and use of textile machinery in the North American colonies for textile production.[82] The machine created by Tully could spin 24 spindles of cotton or wool thread at a time by one person and was similar to England's spinning jenny.[83] English weaver James Hargreaves developed the spinning jenny machine, patented in 1770, for England's thriving cotton textile industry.[84] The purpose of both machines was to increase the number of spindles one person could fill with spun yarn. More spun yarn produced at a time led to the production of more woven cloth. With the use of new machinery, cotton cloth production escalated in Philadelphia. The expansion in cotton production allowed John Hewson to quickly build a reputable fabric printing business as well as a dedicated clientele, which included Martha Washington.[85]

TEXTILE PRODUCTION DURING THE AMERICAN REVOLUTION

During the Revolutionary War, Maryland and Virginia increased their textile production. Elisha and Robert White were successful in setting up a

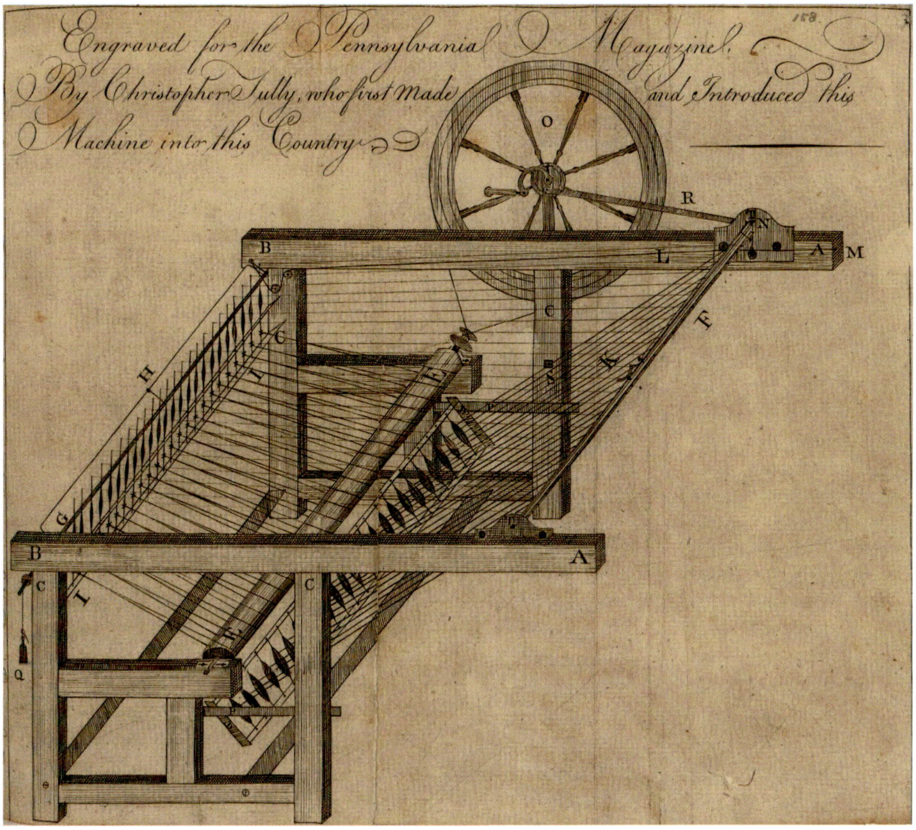

Figure 4.14 Illustration of Christopher Tully's spinning machine. (Christopher Tully, *A New Invented Machine for Spinning of Wool and Cotton*, 1775, engraving, 20.8 x 25.3 cm (8 x 10 in). Courtesy of the John Carter Brown Library.)

fulling mill that could produce mixed cloth of wool and cotton in Hanover County. Lawson McKinny established a fulling mill in Richmond County where fulling, shearing, pressing, and dyeing took place. In Chesterfield County, John Story and Samuel Devenport started a business that fulled, wove, and dyed cloth. Spinning machines for yarn were also being produced in Virginia to help increase cloth production in the region. In Fredericksburg, the partnership of Giles Higson, John Higson, William Paton, Andrew Robinson, and William Wilkie established a company that manufactured a multitude of fabrics as well as sold spinning machines to the general public.[86] The fabrics advertised that could be produced by their company included: jean cloth, velvet, velveret, calico, muslin, striped fabric, corded dimities, corderoy, denim, satinets, linen, checks of all sorts, a variety of woolens, cotton lawn, and silk. To spread the knowledge of textile production, they offered to teach weaving, spinning, shearing, dressing, dyeing, and fulling throughout Virginia. Successful plantation owner Robert Carter III contacted the company in 1777 to build and operate one of the largest cloth manufacturing houses in Virginia.[87]

TEXTILE PRODUCTION AFTER THE AMERICAN REVOLUTION

After the Revolution, there was a concentrated effort on the part of many throughout New England to create a textile manufacturing system equal to Britiain's. While colonists were fighting for independence, the British textile industry boomed with the aid of modern inventions. Richard

Figure 4.15 Johnson's Mill built in 1773 along the Appomattox River. (Timothy H. O'Sullivan and Alexander Gardner, *Johnson's Mill, Petersburg, Virginia*, 1866, photograph, Library of Congress.)

Arkwright established the first water-powered spinning mill in England, with the backing of Jedediah Strutt and Samuel Need. The newly established Cromford Mill used the water frame Arkwright developed specifically to spin cotton yarn. The Cromford water frame could spin 129 spindles at a time while producing strong, coarse yarn that could be used as the warp in manufactured cloth. Very little human labor was needed to operate the machinery.[88] In further developments of the Arkwright water frame, carding and twisting the fibers to prepare them for spinning was done in a single process.[89]

The creation of the Arkwright water frame was followed by the development of the spinning mule, patented in 1779 by Samuel Crompton. The spinning mule could spin 1,000 spindles at a time with one person as the operator. The spinning mule could produce both fine and coarse yarn for the weft and the warp of woven cloth. In 1781, the new Boulton-Watt steam engine, improved by James Watt's with the financial backing of Matthew Boulton, was used to power the spinning mule in the British textile industry. Not only did industrial inventions vastly increase the production of cloth, Thomas Belle's engraved roller printing machine, patented in 1784, sped up the process of cloth printing.[90] A driving force behind the industrialization of the British textile industry in the 18th century was the need to supply the African slave trade. Large quantities of British cotton check fabric were needed for the continued purchase of slaves in Africa. The same British check fabric was also needed to sell to North American slave owners

Figure 4.16 Arkwright's water frame, built in 1775. (Richard Arkwright, *Water frame spinning machine*, 1775, brass, cast iron, leather, wood, and wrought iron, 1170 x 720 x 1400 mm (46 x 28 x 55 in), Science Museum of London. Courtesy of the Science & Society Picture Library.)

to clothe the men, women, and children purchased from slave traders.[91]

Between 1778 and 1789, small textile manufactories were established in Massachusetts, Connecticut, New York, Philadelphia, and Rhode Island.[92] Samuel Whetherill, a former manager of the Philadelphia's American Manufactory, returned to Philadelphia to open his own small textile manufacturing business where he produced jean cloth, fustian, and coatings as well as fulled and dyed fabrics.[93] John Hewson also returned to Philadelphia to reopen his cloth printing business in 1779.[94] In 1787, the 'Pennsylvania Society for the Encouragement of Arts and Domestic Manfactures,' under the leadership of Tench Coxe, reopened the American Manufactory. The factory employed 300 female workers, and was outfitted with a carding machine, four spinning machines with the capacity to spin up to 80 spindles of linen yarn, and eventually 26 looms. As the manufacturing house continued to produce textiles for the public, cotton cloth production was added.[95] John Hewson was contracted to provide bleaching and printing services for the American Manufactory in 1789 as the factory began to focus more on cotton production.[96] In 1787, the first factory established solely for the production of cotton yarn opened in Beverly, Massachusetts, under the supervision of Thomas Somers. In addition to his cotton spinning knowledge, Somers also had experience as a master weaver in the production of dimity, muslins in a variety of checks and stripes, calico, jean cloth, and handkerchief cloth.[97]

Figure 4.17 Carding machine designed by Arkwright in 1800. (Richard Arkright, *Carding engine*, 1800, 1200 x 1220 x 1676 mm (47 x 48 x 66 in), gift of W. Tatham Ltd, Science Museum of London. Courtesy of the Science & Society Picture Library.)

Figure 4.18 The Boulton-Watt steam engine, built in 1788. (James Watt, *Steam Engine*, 1788, cast iron and wood, Science Museum of London. Courtesy of the Science & Society Picture Library.)

Figure 4.19 Early 19th-century calico roller printing machines based on the design created by Thomas Belle. (Thomas Allom, *Calico printing Swainson, Birley & Co cotton mill*, 1834, drawing, 120 mm x 190 mm (4.7 x 7.4 in), Science Museum of London. Courtesy of the Science & Science Picture Library.)

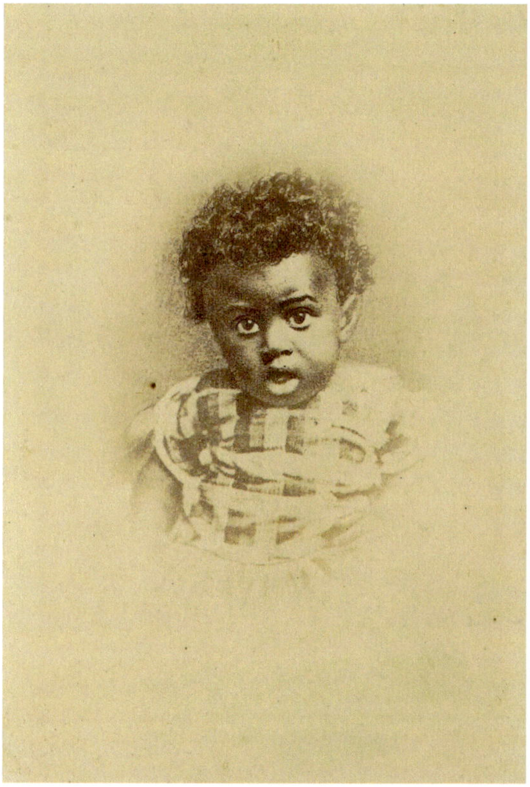

Figure 4.20 Enslaved child photographed in a check shirt. (Matthew Brady, *Young Africa: Or, The Bone of Contention*, 1862, photograph, Library of Congress.)

THE FIRST TEXTILE MILL IN THE UNITED STATES

Despite the efforts to compete with the British textile industry, no one in the northern states had yet mastered textile production incorporating all the technology advances used in Britain. To keep the United States from competing in the textile industry, British law forbade the immigration of anyone with textile manufacturing knowledge or experience. If caught trying to leave for America with manufacturing models, plans, or machines, Britons were heavily fined or imprisoned.[98] 21-year-old Samuel Slater from a family of position in Derbyshire, England, with extensive cotton manufacturing knowledge, knew the consequences but chose to take the risk. At the age of 14, Samuel began an apprenticeship to cotton mill owner Jedediah Strutt, in the hopes of establishing his own mill in the future. As mentioned previously, Strutt partnered with Richard Arkwright in 1771 to establish Cromford Mill, the first water-powered spinning mill in England. In 1779, Strutt and his partner

Samuel Need developed other water-powered cotton mills in Milford and Belper, Derbyshire, close to the Slater family estate. Because of his family's position in the community, Samuel became a management trainee apprentice and one of Strutt's right-hand employees. In his management position, Slater had the opportunity to observe and study all stages of water-powered cotton manufacturing.[99]

During the last years of his apprenticeship, Samuel began to make plans to travel to America to develop his own thriving water-powered textile manufactory. In 1789, dressed as a farm laborer, Samuel boarded a ship bound for America with the knowledge of water-spinning technology in his head.[100] Samuel initially planned to find work in Philadelphia where textile manufacturing was well known to exist. Instead, he took his first job with the New York Manufacturing Company in lower Manhattan.[101] During his time in New York, Slater made the acquaintance of a Captain Brown. Captain Brown owned a ship that sailed from New York to Providence, Rhode Island, on a regular basis and told Slater of merchant Moses Brown, also of Rhode Island. Moses Brown, along with his cousin Smith Brown and his son-in-law William Almy, established the firm Almy & Brown. Together, the three men were determined to create a water-powered spinning mill in Pawtucket, Rhode Island. The partners were in desperate need of someone who had the experience and knowledge of the Arkwright water frame spinning machinery.[102] This series of unexpected events led to the partnership of Almy, Brown, and Slater and the first successful, fully water-powered cotton textile mill in America using water frame technology similar to the Arkwright machinery produced in England.[103]

Figure of 4.21 Slater mill, the first water-powered cotton spinning mill in the United States. (Historic American Engineering record, *Slater Mill, Pawtucket, Providence County, RI.*, 1968, photograph, Library of Congress.)

CHILDREN AND TEXTILE PRODUCTION

The hands behind the operation of the machinery at the newly founded textile mill in Pawtucket were those of children between the ages of seven and 12. Identical to the British textile mill system, Slater employed children to operate the spinning machinery. In the first week of operation in December 1790, Turpin and Charles Arnold, Smith Wilkinson, and Jabez Jenks began full time employment. Eunice and Ann Arnold were soon added to the working crew in the following weeks. Into the third week of operation, a total of seven boys and two girls were employed full time to run the water frame spinning machines six days a week.[104] Fiber spinning was a task that children had been given in the home since the beginning of colonial settlement, which made the transition to working with water-powered spinning machines less difficult for small hands. With the success of water-powered cotton spinning operated by children, Almy, Brown, and Slater agreed the time was right to construct a large mill building in 1792. With the expansion of the Slater mill, the business of Almy, Brown, and Slater now had the capacity to spin, weave, bleach, dye, knit, and finish cloth.[105]

The system of using children in the early textile mills of America is often referred to as 'the Slater system,' although children had been previously employed in textile manufacturing companies and mills located in Beverly and Boston, Massachusetts, New York, Connecticut, and Philadelphia. As the textile industry grew, so did the number of children involved in textile production in the New England

Figure 4.22 Interior first floor of Slater Mill. Spinning mules are located on the right hand side of the photo. A carding machine is located on the left side of the photo. (Historic American Engineering record, *Slater Mill, Pawtucket, Providence County, RI.*, 1968, photograph, Library of Congress.)

mills and on southern plantations.[106] With the success of the Slater mill, more mills began to appear throughout New England. Children who worked in the first mills were children from all social classes, but as time passed, most children working in the mills were from single parent homes or came from struggling agricultural families in nearby communities.[107] Children were also bound out to textile mills through pauper apprenticeships. The percentage of New England girls bound out in pauper apprenticeships rose to 50 percent in the late 18th century as textile manufacturing began to spread.[108] As time progressed, textile mills began to hire entire poor families with a large number of children to operate the machinery or contract with poor parents to employ their children in the operation of the mills.[109] While mill supervisors saw the value in children operating textile machinery, plantation owners saw the value in the labor of enslaved children. By the age of eight, the productivity of slave children on a plantation exceeded the cost of their maintenance.[110] The newly developed textile industry relied on slave children in the South to cultivate cotton and mill children in the North to spin the cotton for cloth production. This economic relationship between plantation owners in the South and textile mill owners in the North was just beginning.

NORTH AND SOUTH TEXTILE PRODUCTION PARTNERSHIP

The development of the cotton mill industry in New England and the need for more child labor coincided with the expansion of Sea Island cotton growth on southern coastal plantations in Georgia and South Carolina. After seeing the rising prices of cotton due to the expanding textile industry in Britain, Georgia planters began growing cotton on the Sea Islands in 1786.[111] Less than 10,000 pounds of Sea Island cotton were produced in 1790, in comparison to a staggering 64 million pounds in 1800.[112] New England textile mills needed large quantities of cotton to produce cloth for the growing new republic. With the development of Eli Whitney's cotton gin in 1793, plantations of short staple cotton, called 'upland cotton,' could now turn a profit in the interior regions of Georgia and South Carolina by sending short staple cleaned cotton to the New England textile mills.[113] Soon after cotton ginning capability spread among southern plantations, Samuel Slater began to supply the Slater mill with southern cotton for cloth production.[114]

Word quickly spread of the need for cotton in the northern textile mills as settlers rushed to find land in the South that could support the

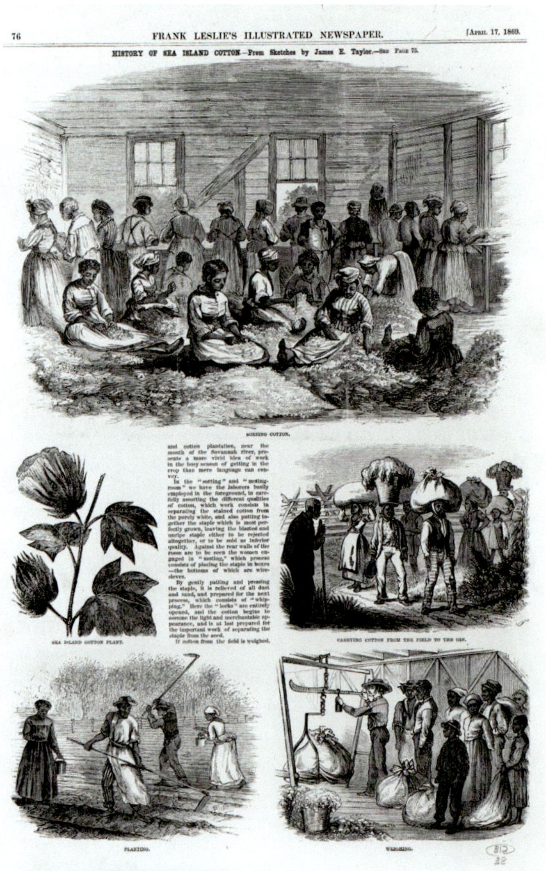

Figure 4.23 (James E. Taylor, *History of Sea Island cotton/from sketches by James E. Taylor*, 1869, wood engraving, Library of Congress.)

Figure 4.24 Illustration detailing the growing stages of the short staple cotton plant. (Nicolas Guerard, *Xilon arboreum J. B. Gossipium orboreum Caule lavi C. B. Pin*, 1732, engraving 18.8 x 14 cm (7.4 x 5.5 in). Courtesy of the John Carter Brown Library.)

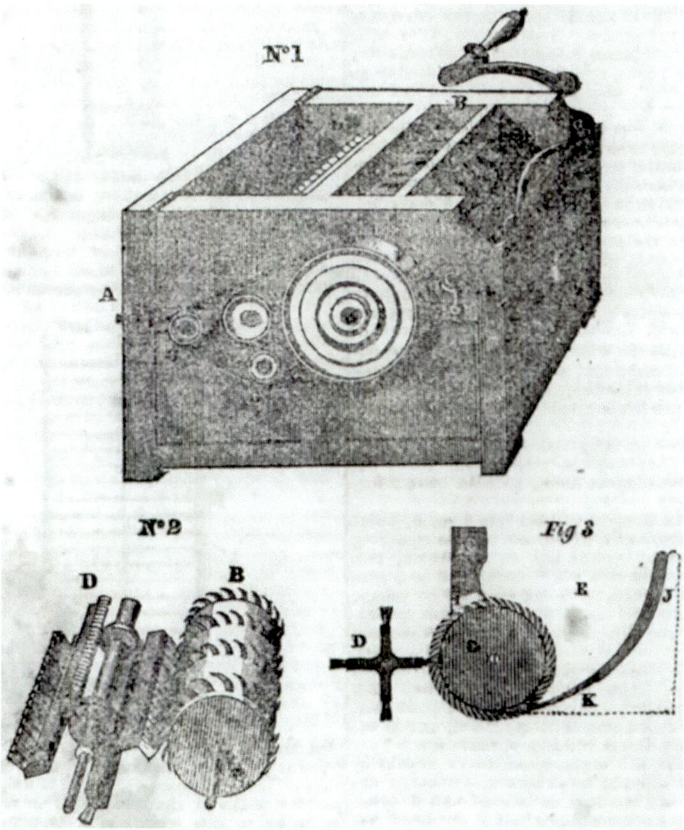

Figure 4.25 Illustration of the cotton gin machine created by Eli Whitney in 1793. (*Cotton Gins . . . the machine invented by Eli Whitney, for ginning cotton, politely sent to us from the U.S. Patent Office*, 1823, woodcut print, Library of Congress.)

cultivation of short staple cotton. The expansion of cotton plantations in the South meant an increase in slave labor. In the 1790s, Georgia's plantation slave labor doubled in population to 60,000 enslaved men, women, and children, while South Carolinas slave population topped 70,000 in the early 19th century.[115] The textile industry in New England became a catalyst for the growing number of enslaved children on plantations now focused on the cultivation of cotton. More than 90,000 enslaved Africans were brought to the United States between the Revolution and the early 19th century. Fifty thousand more were transported and sold in the United States after the African slave trade was legally closed. The rapid increase in slavery was integral in turning southern land, once inhabited by Indigenous people, into a cotton-growing agricultural region that shaped the industrial textile transformation of the Northeast.[116]

In the beginning stages of the American textile industry, in the late 18th century, just as Rhode Island had taken the lead in the African slave trade, Rhode Island was now taking the lead in cotton textile manufacturing. Many of the Rhode Island families who made their wealth through the slave trade were now investing in textile production.[117] Moses Brown came from a successful slave trading family in Rhode Island, but in later years became a Quaker abolitionist. The Browns had been involved in the slave trade beginning in 1736. The Hazard family of southern Rhode Island was another influential slave trading family who became investors in the New England textile industry. With Rowland Hazard's many years of slave trade experience, he saw an opportunity that could tie textile production in the North to cloth needs in the South. Hazard originated the manufacture of 'Negro cloth' in Rhode Island, which supplied southern plantations with cloth to clothe their slave population. Negro cloth in the late 18th century was a cheap, coarse cotton or mixed cotton cloth used to clothe slaves. Low-grade cotton from southern plantations could now supply northern textile mills with the raw material needed to produce large quantities of Negro cloth for the growing slave population. Hazard devised a way to maintain a profit from slavery even as the slave trade was ending.[118]

CLOTHING

REVOLUTIONARY CLOTHING

Before the American Revolution, wearing clothes made of homespun cloth or cloth made in one of the local colonial manufacturing houses was a symbol of resistance to the taxes imposed by the British government on British goods. The 'Daughters of Liberty' made a pact to only wear homespun clothing.[119] A *Massachusetts Gazette* article in 1767 published a poem asking the young women of the community to put aside their London-made brocades and wear instead clothing constructed of country-made linen that was spun by their own hands.[120] The graduating classes of Harvard wore homespun suits to their graduation ceremony in 1768, while the Cambridge graduates wore clothing made from cloth of the local manufacturing houses.[121] The *Boston News Letter* reported a group of 33 women and girls participating in a spinning meeting all wearing homespun dresses of their own making in Rowley, Massachusetts, in June 1769.[122]

Men, women, and children of all social classes were clothing themselves in locally produced cloth. Anna Green Winslow, a 10-year-old schoolgirl in Boston, wrote in her diary that she too considered herself a 'Daughter of Liberty' who chose to wear as much homespun clothing as possible.[123] Colonists throughout Virginia were opting to wear clothing made from homespun cloth in their homes or textiles produced in the local fulling mills.[124] The change of wearing clothing constructed from imported fabrics to colony-made textiles continued throughout the American Revolution. Leading up to, during, and after the

Figure 4.26 Antique thimbles, straight pins, thread, and buttons discovered at George Washington's Mt. Vernon. (Photograph courtesy of the Mount Vernon Ladies' Association.)

Figure 4.27 Boy's late 18th-century silk waistcoat made from a dress worn by Mrs. William Brown. The fabric dates to 1770. (*Waistcoat,* late 18th century, silk, shoulder 10.25; chest 27; waist 26; full length 20 inches. Gift of the estate of Mrs. John D. Murray. Courtesy of the Maryland Center for History and Culture.)

Revolution, households focused their efforts on repairing and reusing garments or fabric, as was practiced in early colonial settlements. A garment was often remodeled multiple times until it became too worn down with time. At that point, the remodeled clothing item was often cut down for a child in the family.[125]

ANGLO-EUROPEAN SMALL CHILDREN'S CLOTHING

In the 18th century, young children were placed in simple dresses, petticoats, and stays. Male and female toddlers were placed in soft muslin frocks with wide necklines.[126] The term 'frock' referred to a younger child's dress that was often fastened in the back.[127] Petticoats for children at this time consisted of a wide waistband with a gathered or pleated skirt attached. A variety of stays were available for small children to wear with their frocks and petticoats. Jumps were a type of supportive bodice or sleeveless waistcoat without rigid boning often worn by boys.[128] A *Pennsylvania Gazette* announcement in 1763 details a small boy's missing shirts, stockings, petticoats, and a pair of jumps.[129] For young girls, stays were traditionally more structured to prepare them for a lifetime of wearing them. Packthread stays for children were made to be more flexible with heavy twine used as the stiffening between the two layers of fabric. Rigid stays were stiffened with whalebone or wooden busks.[130] John McQueen, a stay maker in New York, advertised in 1767 that he carried packthread stays, whalebone stays, and jumps for children in his shop.[131]

Figure 4.28 Front view of child's fancy dress coat made in the early 19th century from 18th-century fabric. (*Coat*, early 19th century, silk brocade, silk satin, cotton flannel, shoulder 13; chest 28; waist 24; hips 30; neck to waist 15; full length 30.5 inches. Bequest of Ellin Curzon Pleasants. Courtesy of the Maryland Center for History and Culture.)

Figure 4.29 Back view of child's fancy dress coat made in the early 19th century from 18th-century fabric. (*Coat*, early 19th century, silk brocade, silk satin, cotton flannel, shoulder 13; chest 28; waist 24; hips 30; neck to waist 15; full length 30.5 inches. Bequest of Ellin Curzon Pleasants. Courtesy of the Maryland Center for History and Culture.)

Figure 4.30 Waistband and pleated skirt detail of a child's homespun petticoat worn by a member of the Wood family of Duxbury, Massachusetts, in the third quarter of the 18th century. (*Petticoat*, 1775, linen and cotton, waistband 3 ¼ x 18; pleats ½ inch. Gift of Cynthia Chapman Woodard, 1875. Courtesy of the Duxbury and Rural Historical Society.)

Figure 4.31 Back view of child's homespun petticoat with hand-printed trim worn by a member of the Wood family of Duxbury, Massachusetts, in the third quarter of the 18th century. (*Petticoat*, 1775, linen and cotton, waist 18; top of waistband to hem 18 ½; trim width 1 inch. Gift of Cynthia Chapman Woodard, 1875. Courtesy of the Duxbury and Rural Historical Society.)

Figure 4.32 Inside view of a pair of homespun infant stays worn by a member of the Wood family of Duxbury, Massachusetts, in the third quarter of the 18th century. (*Infant stays*, 1775, 6 ¼ x 19 ¾ in (15.8 x 50.1 cm), gift of Cynthia Chapman Woodard, 1875. Courtesy of the Duxbury and Rural Historical Society.)

ANGLO-EUROPEAN BOYS' CLOTHING

Just before the American Revolution, the stages of clothing a boy from toddler age to the early teenage years were simplified in comparison to the early 18th century. Toddler boys transitioned from a dress or frock with petticoats and stays to a pair of long trousers called pantaloons at the breeching age. The pantaloons were worn with a shirt and often a short jacket.[132] The straight leg pantaloons boys began to wear initially did not have a fall front construction. As boys grew and could manage buttoning and unbuttoning a fall front pant, they were then placed in fall front pantaloons. In the later years of the 18th century, young boys were often seen in fall front overalls with a shirt and short jacket.[133] Nankeen was a favored fabric for boys' clothing before and after the Revolution. Nankeen was a tan cotton fabric used to make breeches, overalls, jackets, and suits for boys. It was worn throughout the seasons of the year, except for extremely cold weather, and was worn by all social classes.[134] The pantaloon stage for young boys was then followed by a modified adult look.[135]

The suit coat of an older boy followed the long cutaway style of adult men with set in slim sleeves finished off by a moderate-width cuff. Front pockets with flaps were also popular in suit coats for older boys and men. Underneath the suit coat, a boy was clothed in a full-sleeved shirt with fabric frills at the neck and often the wrist. Over the shirt, just like adult men, an older boy wore a long, button front waistcoat often constructed with front flap pockets. A boy's suit

Figure 4.33 Red-striped dress worn by Ebenezer Johnson, son of Captain William Pierce Johnson of Newburyport, Massachusetts. (*Dress*, 1795–1798, vermilion, ocher, black and gold silk weave; lace collar and cuffs; white linen lining. From the collections of the Museum of Old Newbury.)

Figure 4.34 Front view of a pair of boy's cotton nankeen overalls with a matching jacket. (*Overalls and jacket*, 1795–1810, cotton nankeen, overall bib height 3.5; waist 19; waist to hem 19 inches. Courtesy of Historic New England.)

Figure 4.35 Close up detail of the nankeen overall's fall front construction. (*Overalls*, 1795–1810, cotton nankeen with coarse linen lining, bib height 3.5; fall front width 7; fall front depth 4 inches. Courtesy of Historic New England.)

at this stage was paired with breeches instead of pantaloons. The breeches were also fall front construction with side openings at the bottom of the leg that were finished off with a small band. Knee buckles or buttons were used to close the breeches at the knee of the wearer. Depending on the social class of the boy, the clothing pieces of a mid-18th century suit could be made from simple homespun fabric or costly satin. In the portrait of 10-year-old Thomas Chamberlaine, painted by John Hesselius, Thomas is wearing a suit comprised of a cutaway coat with a bit of fullness in the back and decorated with a series of buttons along both sides of the open front coat. In addition to the suit coat, Thomas is clothed in a high-collared shirt with ruffles at the wrists and chest. Over the shirt, he is wearing a long line waistcoat with front flap pockets. The portrait ends just before the hem of Thomas's coat and waistcoat. If the image of the portrait continued, the viewer would be able to see the breeches that were paired with the suit.

At the end of the 18th century, older boys' long line suit coats became slimmer in silhouette. They were often double-breasted and constructed

Figure 4.36 Back view of boy's nankeen overalls and matching jacket. (*Overalls and matching jacket*, 1795–1810, cotton nankeen, overall bib height 3.5; waist 19; waist to hem 19 inches. Courtesy of Historic New England.)

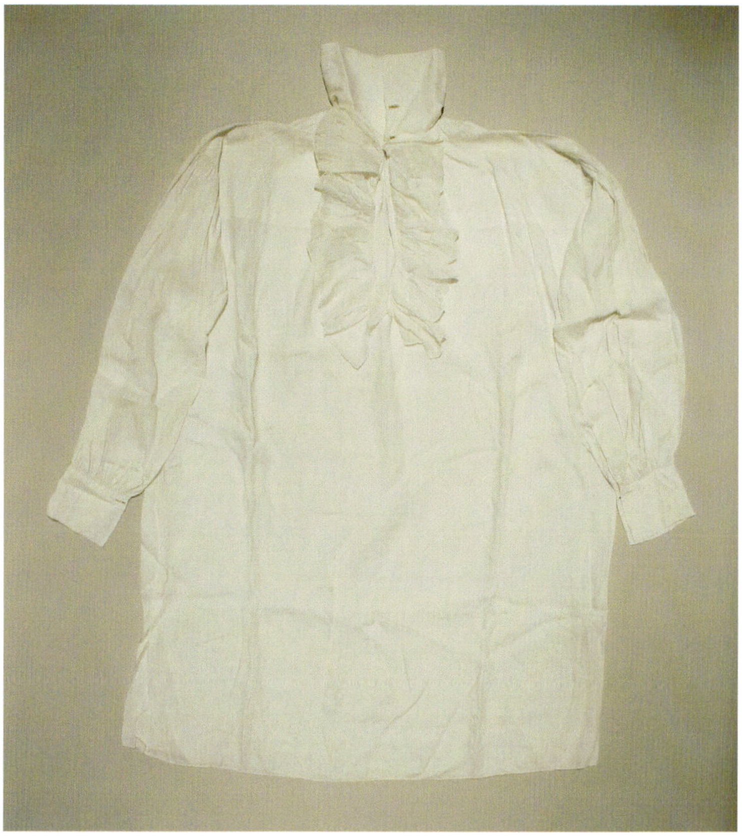

Figure 4.37 Boy's 18th-century linen shirt. (*Shirt,* 18th century, linen, gift of Mr. Claggett Wilson, 1941. Courtesy of The Metropolitan Museum of Art.)

Figure 4.38 Portrait of Thomas Chamberlaine III. (John Hesselius, Thomas Chamberlaine, III, 1772–1775, oil on canvas, 74.6 x 61.9 cm (29 3/8 x 24 3/8 in), gift of Dexter M. Ferry Jr., 44.140. Courtesy of the Detroit Institute of Arts.)

Figure 4.39 Boy's 18th-century striped cotton suit coat. (*Coat,* 1700–1799, cotton, gift of Judith and Ira L. Sommer, 1895. Courtesy of The Metropolitan Museum of Art.)

Figure 4.40 A pair of boy's red wool breeches worn by Daniel Arnold in 1761. (Breeches, 1761, wool, gift of the Brooklyn Museum, 2009. Courtesy of The Metropolitan Museum of Art.)

Figure 4.41 A boy's cream dimity double-breasted suit jacket and matching pantaloons with hand printed trim. (*Boy's suit in two pieces*, late 18th century, dimity and cotton, pantaloon buttoned waistband height 4 ½; waist 24; waist seam to hem 21 in; jacket shoulder to hem 12 ½; chest 24 in, gift of Aimee and Rosamund Lamb, 1951. Courtesy of Museum of Fine Arts, Boston.)

with a high back collar and wide lapels. The tail portion of the coat was squared off in the back. Waistcoats were short, double-breasted and often cut with a high collar and large lapels, similar to the suit coat. In contrast, younger boy's suit coats or jackets were cut short without a tail but followed the double-breasted trend worn by men and older boys. While small boys wore pantaloons with their shortened-style, double-breasted suit coats, older boys often wore breeches.[136] Indigenous boys bound as apprentices or servants were dressed in a variation of shirts, jackets, overalls, and breeches, similar to male adult servants or laborers. An Indigenous teenage boy ran away from his master in Rhode Island wearing a gray coat with pewter buttons, leather breeches, and a tow shirt.[137] According to an announcement in the *Pennsylvania Gazette*, in 1778 an indentured mulatto servant ran away with her six-year-old son who was wearing a brown cloth coat and a pair of osnaburg overalls.[138]

ANGLO-EUROPEAN GIRLS' CLOTHING

After 1770, girls transitioned from a dress or frock, petticoats and more structured stays into modified adult women's clothing at an early age. While a boy in the later 18th century went through three phases of dress, a girl only had two.[139] Although a young girl had fewer stages of clothing, there were several styles of dress options to choose from. The popular robe-style mantua of the earlier 18th century was still worn before, during, and just after the American Revolution by small female children through

Figure 4.42 Portrait of Mrs. Noah Smith and her children of Bolton, Connecticut, dated 1798. The oldest son is wearing appropriate attire for older boys in the late 18th century. (Ralph Earl, *Mrs. Noah Smith and Her Children*, 1798, oil on canvas, 64 x 85 3/4 in (162.6 x 217.8 cm), gift of Edgar Wiliam and Bernice Chrysler Garbisch, 1962. Courtesy of The Metropolitan Museum of Art.)

to adult women. Mantuas could be constructed of simple homespun cloth or more elaborate silks and satins. Most professional mantua makers in the 18th century were women. In addition to mantuas, mantua makers could create custom gowns, petticoats, and undergarments for their female clientele.[140] Mantua makers, whose clients requested a custom order, often cut the garment in the client's home. In her 18th century diary, a Philadelphia resident, Elizabeth Drinker, recorded employing the services of dressmaker Betsy Fordham. From the writings of Elizabeth's journal, Betsy cut, fit, and completed the fine detail work for a new gown, while Elizabeth sewed the simpler seams.[141]

Another style of dress for young girls was a bodice connected to an overskirt that was open in the front. Under the bodice and split-front overskirt was often a Marseilles quilted petticoat. Marseilles quilted petticoats were constructed with a woven cotton or linen as the backing and a satin or plain weave fabric for the front. The intricate needlework design of the petticoat was drawn on the underside of the backing fabric. The two fabrics were joined together by a running stitch or back stitch that outlined the drawn pattern. Once the two fabrics were sewn together, cotton batting was used to stuff particular areas of the stitched design to give a dimensional look

Figure 4.43 Mrs. Jacob Hurd and her child. Mrs. Jacob is wearing a front-opening mantua with a stomacher pinned to her corset. Her child is wearing a dress, under petticoats, and a pair of stays. (William Johnston, *Mrs. Jacob Hurd and Child*, 1762, oil on canvas, 30 x 25 in. (76.2 x 63.5 cm). Courtesy of The Metropolitan Museum of Art.)

Figure 4.44 Front view of a child's homespun linen mantua worn by a member of the Wood family of Duxbury, Massachusetts, in the third quarter of the 18th century. (*Dress*, 1775, linen and cotton, bodice length 6 ¼; waist 20 inches; skirt length 15 ¼; neck edge to hem 21 ½ inches. Gift of Cynthia Chapman Woodard, 1875. Courtesy of the Duxbury and Rural Historical Society.)

Figure 4.45 Close up of a child's homespun mantua. (*Dress*, 1775, linen and cotton, bodice length 6 ¼; waist 20 inches; skirt length 15 ¼; neck edge to hem 21 ½ inches. Gift of Cynthia Chapman Woodard, 1875. Courtesy of the Duxbury and Rural Historical Society.)

Figure 4.46 Back view of a child's homespun mantua. (*Dress*, 1775, linen and cotton, bodice length 6 ¼; waist 20 inches; skirt length 15 ¼; neck edge to hem 21 ½ inches. Gift of Cynthia Chapman Woodard, 1875. Courtesy of the Duxbury and Rural Historical Society.)

Figure 4.47 A Marseilles quilted petticoat. (*Petticoat*, 1750–1799, silk, gift of The New York Historical Society, 1979. Courtesy of The Metropolitan Museum of Art.)

to the finished quilted petticoat.[142] Decorative aprons were also worn over the split-front overskirt and quilted petticoat. At a ball hosted by Virginia plantation owner Robert Carter, Phillip Vickers Fithian, the tutor for the Carter family, described 15-year-old Ms. Hale wearing a white holland dress, a cotton quilted petticoat, and a fine lawn apron.[143]

As girls from elite social classes grew close to their teenage years, stays became more structured and tighter in construction. The 'appropriate' silhouette of a wealthy young female at this time was an incredibly straight posture and narrow chest. Extremely rigid stays for girls, in order to keep their posture erect and their stature small, were constructed of a wooden board placed in the front and back of a tightly sewn buckram jacket, which was additionally reinforced with whalebone and sometimes metal.[144] A young schoolgirl from a wealthy family often spent part of her day each day in these inflexible garments.[145] Girls were also taught to sit with their heads held high while they studied or sewed. The stay maker John McQueen also advertised neatly polished steel collars for young girls in boarding schools to wear. The style of collar he sold was similar to those worn in Britain by elite school-age girls.[146] These 'training' garments were used to prepare young girls to marry well in Upper-class social circles. It was common in the 18th century for girls to marry by the age of 15.[147]

Toward the end of the Revolution, clothing for girls simplified. In John Singleton Copley's painting *Young Lady with a Bird and a Dog*, Copley captures a small girl in a pink dress with a square-cut bodice attached to a finely gathered skirt. The elbow-length sleeves are set into a narrow shoulder and finished off with a white lace. The under chemise the young girl is wearing can be seen at the top of the square neckline as well as below the bottom of the lace-edged sleeve where it has been tied with a dark-blue ribbon at the elbow. The waist of the bodice is cut straight across and ends a few inches below the child's natural waist. The only trim visible is a gold lace that outlines the square neckline of the dress. These simple dresses were often seen with a wide sash across the front that tied in a large bow at the back. This style of dress became the preferred fashion for girls until the last years of the 18th century.[148] The dresses were created in fine fabrics as well as homespun textiles. In a home that was repurposing and reusing older fabrics for clothing items, this style of dress could be made from cloth woven before the Revolutionary War. As the 18th century progressed, the waistlines of these dresses began to rise higher on the wearer.

At the end of the 18th century, dresses for both young boys and young girls became even more simplistic. A streamline frock or dress was cut similar to an under shift with short sleeves and no waist seam. The garment could either fall over the child with no cinching at the waist, or a drawstring construction was placed inside the garment in order to cinch the fabric to the child, just under the chest. This drawstring variation created a high-waisted effect on both boys and girls.[149] Another variation of the streamlined frock was constructed with fabric ties placed on either side of the simple gown that were tied together at the back of the child. These dresses could have long or short sleeves, depending on the season and were made from a variety of fabrics. Wealthier children's dresses were

Figure 4.48 (John Singleton Copley, *Young Lady with a Bird and Dog*, 1767, oil on canvas, 122 x 101 cm (48 X 39.7 in), purchased with funds from the Florence Scott Libbey Bequest in Memory of her Father, Maurice A. Scott, 1950.306. Courtesy of the Toledo Museum of Art.)

Figure 4.49 Child's cotton dress constructed similarly to the young girl's dress in Figure 4.48. (*Dress*, 1762–1786, cotton, gift of the Brooklyn Museum, 2009. Courtesy of The Metropolitan Museum of Art.)

Figure 4.50 Late 18th-century child's dress pieced together from homespun, hand-printed linen created earlier in the 18th century. (Photograph courtesy of Old Sturbridge Village, Sturbridge, Massachusetts.)

made of fine muslin, while poorer children's dresses were made of coarser fabrics.

An additional clothing item a child could wear with the late-18th century simple style of dress was a short gown. Servant women, pregnant women, or women engaged in physical labor in their homes wore short gowns. A short gown for young girls was shaped similarly to a child's open front mantua with long sleeves and no waist seam. The short gown was loosely cut to mid-thigh on the wearer. When worn by women, the open front of the short gown was pinned shut and cinched to the body by the ties of an apron that were placed over the jacket like garment.[150] Indigenous and mixed-race girls bound out as apprentices or servants were clothed in plain garments similar to female servants and laborers, which often included a simple dress and short gown.[151]

AFRICAN ENSLAVED CHILDREN'S CLOTHING

In the 1760s, taxes imposed on textiles by the British government also affected the clothing of slaves. South Carolina politician Ralph Izzard wrote to southern plantation owner Henry Laurens concerning trade relationships with Britain. Izzard's concern centered on the importation of textiles used to clothe slaves in South Carolina. If buying textiles for slave clothing from Britain was no longer an option, southern plantation owners needed to find another way to clothe their slaves.[152]

Figure 4.51 Portrait of Lucy Knapp Mygatt and son, George. (John Brewster Jr., *Mother and Son*, 1799, oil on canvas, 54 ¼ x 40 in (137.7 x 101.6 cm), gift of Mrs. Nancy Adams McCord. Courtesy of Palmer Museum of Art).

Not only did London provide durable textiles for clothing slaves, several London companies made garments for the enslaved that could be shipped directly to plantation owners. James Habersham, a merchant, slave trader, and slave owner in Georgia, wrote a letter in 1764 detailing an order for a large quantity of slave clothing. He was writing on behalf of himself, the Governor of Georgia, and a Mr. Harris. Habersham's order included 120 male jackets and breeches as well as 80 female dresses in a variety of sizes.[153] If trade was disrupted with Britain, as Izzard feared, textiles and clothing for enslaved men, women, and children needed to be locally sourced.

As the American Revolution neared, trade was disrupted with Britain. In 1775, Izzard began growing a large quantity of cotton on his plantation for the purpose of clothing his slaves.[154] Plantation owners began organizing spinning and weaving activities on their plantations in order to clothe the enslaved members of their estate as well as their family members. George Washington built a spinning house for cloth production to clothe his large population of slaves, family members, and surrounding neighbors. To oversee the production of textiles at Mount Vernon, he hired a woman from the community to oversee five enslaved girls in the spinning and weaving process.[155] In addition to spinning and weaving, a group of eight to ten female slaves in the late 18th century also made clothing for the population at Mount Vernon.[156] Enslaved children were often assigned to textile and clothing production on plantations as well as in smaller homes owned by their masters. Susan Matthews, a small, enslaved child in Georgia, was raised by her master's wife, even though her mother was also a slave in the household. Susan slept at the foot of her mistress's bed to keep her owner's feet warm at night. During the day, Susan first learned to sew by making clothes for the doll she was given by her mistress. This led to a lifetime of sewing for her master's family and the other slaves in the household.[157]

As styles changed in fashion for the Upper and middle classes in the 18th century, slaves remained simply and plainly dressed by their masters. Louisa Piquet described in her narrative wearing two pieces of clothing in the summer, an underdress and an overdress made of a blue-striped homespun fabric, specifically woven for slaves in Georgia.[158] While some masters provided adequate clothing for their enslaved men, women, and children in the mid to late 18th century, others did not. In his 18th century journal, Virginia plantation owner William Byrd II disapproved of how the master of the Jones' plantation clothed his slaves. According to Byrd's writings, the men, women, and children on the plantation were scantily clad.[159] In his personal journal, Ebenezer Hazard spoke of his dismay to see slave children so poorly clothed. Hazard

Figure 4.52 Child's late 18th century simple block printed shift with inner drawstring construction. (*Shift*, 1780–1810, undyed linen with a small red dot vermicelli pattern, neck front to hem 19; waist 19 inches. Gift of the New England Historic Genealogical Society. Courtesy of Historic New England.)

served as a postmaster during the Revolutionary War, assigned in 1777 to organize a postal route from Philadelphia to Savannah. While mapping out a safe postal route, Hazard spent time in the rural parts of Virginia as well as the capital city of Williamsburg. Hazard recorded the astonishing lack of clothing enslaved boys wore. He described boys between the ages of ten to 12 as either quite naked or only having a shirt that hung part way down their backs. The sight was so commonplace in Virginia, the genteel women in the communities seemed not to take notice of what Hazard felt was a shocking sight.[160] As the Industrial Revolution moved forward with the large-scale production of Negro cloth in the early 19th century, slave owners had the opportunity to clothe their enslaved children in proper garments. Unfortunately, as we have seen, in the 18th century, the lack of clothing continued for enslaved boys and girls in the 19th century.

The experiences of children in colonial America and the newly formed United States depended on the social and economic class they were assigned to. Children in higher social positions had access to education and financial security. Impoverished children were reliant on what systems were in place to address poverty in their communities. Indigenous children were caught in a system of colonial government that saw more value in the land they inhabited than the children themselves. Plantation owners harnessed the labor of enslaved African children with the development of a textile industry that heavily relied on the mass production of cotton. The success of the American textile industry was possible through the labor of enslaved children in the South and the mill children of the

Figure 4.53 Child's simple striped and hand-printed late 18th-century dress with a remaining waist tie. (*Dress*, late 18th century, cotton, neck front to hem 20; chest 21; hem circumference 59 inches. Photograph courtesy of Old Sturbridge Village, Sturbridge, Massachusetts.)

Figure 4.54 Child's late 18th-century simple block-printed shift with matching short gown. (*Shift and Short Gown*, 1780–1810, undyed linen with small red dot vermicelli pattern, gift of the New England Historic Genealogical Society. Courtesy of Historic New England.)

Figure 4.55 Spinning room at George Washington's Mt. Vernon. (*The Spinning room at Mt. Vernon*, 1910–1920, photograph, *Detroit Publishing Company*, Library of Congress.)

Figure 4.56 Captured African men, women, and children sold into slavery on the shore of the United States. (*United States slave trade*, 1830, engraving on woven paper, 10 x 17 cm (4 x 6.6 in), Library of Congress.)

North. Children of all social classes were dressed in homespun clothing as the colonies fought for their independence from Britain. With a shift in fabrics, there also came a shift in the silhouette of children's clothing. As the 18th century ended, clothing for children simplified. The economic status of the child determined what fabrics were used in the construction of the garments and how many clothing items the child was given to wear.

NOTES

1 Richard Middleton and Anne Lombard, *Colonial America: A History to 1763*, 4th ed. (West Sussex: Wiley-Blackwell, 2011), 443–44.

2 Gloria McCahon Whiting, "Race, Slavery, and the Problem of Numbers in Early New England: A View from Probate Court," *The William and Mary Quarterly* 77, no. 3 (2020): 413.

3 Kathleen A. Staples and Madelyn Shaw, *Clothing Through American History* (Oxford: Greenwood, 2013), 154.

4 E. H. Cameron, *Samuel Slater Father of American Manufactures* (Portland: The Bond Wheelwright Company, 1960), 4–6.

5 Edith Abbott, "A Study of the Early History of Child Labor in America," *American Journal of Sociology* 14, no. 1 (1908): 22–24, www.jstor.org/stable/2762758.

6 Karin Cavert, *Children in the House: The Material Culture of Early Childhood, 1600–1900* (Boston: Northeastern University Press, 1992), 92; Estelle Ansley Worrell, *Children's Costume in America 1607–1910* (New York: Charles Scribner's Sons, 1980), 41.

7 Staples and Shaw, *Clothing Through American History*, 401; Ebenezer Hazard and Fred Shelley, "The Journal of Ebenezer Hazard in Virginia, 1777," *The Virginia Magazine of History and Biography* 62, no. 4 (1954): 410, www.jstor.org/stable/4246052.

8 James Marten, ed., *Children in Colonial America* (New York: New York University Press, 2007), 106–10.

9 Marten, *Children in Colonial America*, 106–10.

10 David Hackett Fischer, *Albion's Seed: Four British Folkways in America* (New York: Oxford University Press, 1989), 311–17.

11 Fischer, *Albion's Seed*, 311–17.

12 Fischer, 347–48.

13 Ruth Wallis Herndon and John E. Murray, eds., *Children Bound to Labor: The Pauper Apprentice System in Early America* (Ithaca: Cornell University Press, 2009), 184–96.

14 Herndon and Murray, *Children Bound to Labor*, 10.

15 Lyon G. Tyler, "Education in Colonial Virginia: Part I, Poor Children and Orphans," *The William and Mary Quarterly* 5, no. 4 (1897): 223, https://doi.org/10.2307/1914924.

16 Herndon and Murray, 191.

17 Tim Lockley, "Rural Poor Relief in Colonial South Carolina," *The Historical Journal* 48, no. 4 (2005): 957, www.jstor.org/stable/4091644.

18 Lockley, "Rural Poor Relief," 957, 963, 966–69.

19 Lockley, 957, 963, 966–69.

20 Herndon and Murray, 104; John E. Murray and Ruth Wallis Herndon, "Markets for Children in Early America: A Political Economy of Pauper Apprenticeship," *The Journal of Economic History* 62, no. 2 (2002): 360, www.jstor.org/stable/2698184.

21 Roxanne Dunbar-Ortiz, *An Indigenous Peoples' History of the United States* (Boston: Beacon Press, 2014), 74.

22 Dunbar-Ortiz, *An Indigenous Peoples' History*, 75.

23 Dunbar-Ortiz, 75; Laurence French and Jim Hornbuckle, eds., "The Cherokees – Then and Now," in *The Cherokee Perspective: Written by Eastern Cherokees* (Appalachian State University, 1981), 16, https://doi.org/10.2307/j.ctt1xp3kws.7.

24 Edward Countryman, "Indians, the Colonial Order, and the Social Significance of the American Revolution," *The William and Mary Quarterly* 53, no. 2 (1996): 358, https://doi.org/10.2307/2947405.

25 Brenden Kennedy, "'Not Worth a Pinch of Snuff': The 1789 Yazoo Land Sale and Sovereignty in the Old Southwest," *The Georgia Historical Quarterly* 101, no. 3 (2017): 199, www.jstor.org/stable/44651786.

26 Kennedy, "Not Worth a Pinch of Snuff," 199.

27 French and Hornbuckle, "The Cherokees – Then and Now," 15.

28 John Craig Hammond, "Slavery, Settlement, and Empire: The Expansion and Growth of Slavery in the Interior of the North American Continent, 1770–1820," *Journal of the Early Republic* 32, no. 2 (2012): 179, www.jstor.org/stable/41478766.

29 Paul M. Pressly, "Scottish Merchants and the Shaping of Colonial Georgia," *The Georgia Historical Quarterly* 91, no. 2 (2007): 144–46, www.jstor.org/stable/40584995.

30 Darold D. Wax, "Georgia and the Negro Before the American Revolution," *The Georgia Historical Quarterly* 51, no. 1 (1967): 74, www.jstor.org/stable/40578875; Pressly, "Scottish Merchants," 144–46.

31 David Brown and Clive Webb, *Race in the American South: From Slavery to Civil Rights* (Edinburgh University Press, 2007), 63, www.jstor.org/stable/10.3366/j.ctt1g0b353.
32 Sven Beckert, *Empire of Cotton* (New York: Vintage Books, 2015), 101.
33 Wilma King, *African American Childhoods: Historical Perspectives from Slavery to Civil Rights* (New York: Palgrave Macmillan, 2005), 12–13.
34 Sheila Flemming-Hunter, "Project 1619 Revisited: Black Children, Racism, and Reparations," *Phylon (1960–)* 57, no. 1 (2020): 80, www.jstor.org/stable/26924988.
35 Winthrop D. Jordan, "The Influence of the West Indies on the Origins of New England Slavery," *The William and Mary Quarterly* 18, no. 2 (1961): 246–49, https://doi.org/10.2307/1918546.
36 Spencer R. Crew, Lonnie G. Bunch III, and Clement A. Price, eds., *Memories of the Enslaved: Voices from the Slave Narratives* (Santa Barbara: Praeger, 2015), 56.
37 Flemming-Hunter, "Project 1619 Revisited," 80.
38 Crew, Bunch, and Price, *Memories of the Enslaved*, 43.
39 Crew, Bunch, and Price, 67.
40 Marten, 204.
41 Marten, 204–5, 213.
42 Marten, 204.
43 Susan Borrows Swan, *Plain and Fancy: American Women and Their Needlework, 1700–1850* (New York: Routledge, 1977), 46–55.
44 Swan, *Plain and Fancy*, 46–60, 88.
45 Swan, 46–60, 88.
46 Marten, 164.
47 Murray and Herndon, "Markets for Children in Early America," 365–67.
48 Murray and Herndon, 365–67.
49 Murray and Herndon, 375.
50 Herndon and Murray, 39–44.
51 Marten, 205.
52 Daniel R. Mandell, *Tribe, Race, History: Native Americans in Southern New England 1780–1880* (Baltimore: John Hopkins University Press, 2007), 28.
53 Countryman, "Indians, the Colonial Order, and the Social Significance of the American Revolution," 358.
54 Dunbar-Ortiz, 77.
55 Hammond, "Slavery, Settlement, and Empire," 175.
56 Leonardo Marques, "Slave Trading in a New World: The Strategies of North American Slave Traders in the Age of Abolition," *Journal of the Early Republic* 32, no. 2 (2012): 235, www.jstor.org/stable/41478768.
57 Marques, "Slave Trading in a New World," 240.
58 Jared Ross Hardesty, *Black Lives, Native Lands, White Worlds: A History of Slavery in New England* (Boston, MA: Bright Leaf, 2019), 135.
59 Emily Blanck, "Seventeen Eighty-Three: The Turning Point in the Law of Slavery and Freedom in Massachusetts," *The New England Quarterly* 75, no. 1 (2002): 24, https://doi.org/10.2307/1559880.
60 Herndon and Murray, 43.
61 Herndon and Murray, 43, 50.
62 Mandell, *Tribe, Race, History*, 28.
63 Murray and Herndon, 370.
64 Carter G. Woodson, "The Negro in New England," *Negro History Bulletin* 5, no. 1 (1941): 6, www.jstor.org/stable/44246616.
65 Whiting, "Race, Slavery, and the Problem of Numbers in Early New England," 413.
66 Herndon and Murray, 43.
67 Abbott, "A Study of the Early History of Child Labor in America," 19.
68 Staples and Shaw, 154.
69 William R. Bagnall, *The Textile Industries of the United States*, vol. 1 (Cambridge: Riverside Press, 1893), 50–53, Google Books.
70 Staples and Shaw, 154.
71 Bagnall, *The Textile Industries of the United States*, 56.
72 Bagnall, 53.
73 Laurel Thatcher Ulrich, *The Age of Homespun: Objects and Stories in the Creation of an American Myth* (New York: Vintage Books, 2001), 176.
74 Ulrich, *The Age of Homespun*, 176.
75 Bagnall, 58.
76 Ulrich, 178.
77 Marten, 207.
78 Bagnall, 48.
79 Max Hamrick, *Organic Fiber Dyeing: The Colonial Williamsburg Method* (Paducah: American Quilter's Society, 2013), 20.
80 Kimberly Wulfert, "The Man of Many Vases: John Hewson Calico Printer," *Folk Art* (Fall 2007): 60.
81 Bagnall, 63–72.
82 Bagnall, 63–72.
83 Bagnall, 63–72.
84 Mary Schoeser and Celia Rufey, *English and American Textiles: From 1790 to the Present* (New York: Thames and Hudson, 1989), 29.
85 Nancy Andrews Reath, "A Philadelphia Calico-Printer," *Bulletin of the Pennsylvania Museum* 26, no. 138 (1931): 27, https://doi.org/10.2307/3794418.

86 Hamrick, *Organic Fiber Dyeing*, 23–30.
87 Hamrick, 23–30.
88 Schoeser and Rufey, *English and American Textiles*, 29–30.
89 Virginia Postrel, *The Fabric of Civilization: How Textiles Made the World* (New York: Basic Books, 2020), 66.
90 Schoeser and Rufey, 29–30.
91 Ronald Bailey, "The Other Side of Slavery: Black Labor, Cotton, and Textile Industrialization in Great Britain and the United States," *Agricultural History* 68, no. 2 (1994): 43, www.jstor.org/stable/3744401.
92 Cameron, *Samuel Slater Father of American Manufactures*, 11.
93 Bagnall, 72.
94 Wulfert, "The Man of Many Vases," 61.
95 Bagnall, 79.
96 Wulfert, 61.
97 Bagnall, 90.
98 Cameron, 4–6.
99 Cameron, 4–6.
100 Cameron, 30.
101 Cameron, 35.
102 Cameron, 35–37.
103 Cameron, 25.
104 Cameron, 58.
105 Cameron, 25.
106 Abbott, 22–24.
107 Gary Kulik, Roger Parks, and Theodore Z. Penn, eds., *The New England Mill Village, 1790–1860*, vol. 2 (Cambridge: The MIT Press, 1982), xxix.
108 Herndon and Murray, 48.
109 Herndon and Murray, 203.
110 Herndon and Murray, 202.
111 Beckert, *Empire of Cotton*, 101.
112 Beckert, 102.
113 Beckert, 103.
114 Cameron, 59.
115 Beckert, 103.
116 Countryman, 361.
117 David Roediger and Martin H. Blatt, *The Meaning of Slavery in the North* (New York: Garland Publishing, Inc., 1998), 15, 37.
118 Roediger and Blatt, *The Meaning of Slavery in the North*, 15, 37.
119 Cecil Lubell, *Textile Collections of the World: United States and Canada*, vol. 1 (New York: Van Nostrand Reinhold Company, 1976), 131.
120 Bagnall, 57.
121 Lubell, *Textile Collections of the World*, 131; Bagnall, 56.
122 Bagnall, 57.
123 Alice Morse Earle, *Two Centuries of Costume in America: 1620–1820*, vol. 1 (Williamstown: Corner House Publishers, 1974), 299.
124 Mary Newton Standard, *Colonial Virginia Its People and Customs* (Philadelphia: J. B. Lippincott Company, 1917), 205, Google Books.
125 Swan, 19.
126 Worrell, *Children's Costume in America*, 35.
127 Noreen Marshall, *Dictionary of Children's Clothes: 1700s to Present* (London: V & A Publishing, 2008), 104.
128 Staples and Shaw, 384.
129 *Pennsylvania Gazette*, March 24, 1763.
130 Edward Warwick, Henry C. Pitz, and Alexander Wyckoff, *Early American Dress: The Colonial and Revolutionary Periods* (New York: Bonanza Books, 1965), 239.
131 Earle, *Two Centuries of Costume in America*, 316.
132 Cavert, *Children in the House*, 92.
133 Warwick, Pitz, and Wyckoff, *Early American Dress*, 243.
134 Alice Morse Earle, *Costume of Colonial Times* (New York: Charles Scribner's Sons, 1894), 166.
135 Cavert, 92.
136 Worrell, 47.
137 Staples and Shaw, 401.
138 *Pennsylvania Gazette*, October 15, 1778.
139 Cavert, 92.
140 Staples and Shaw, 191.
141 Swan, 23.
142 Swan, 154.
143 Standard, *Colonial Virginia Its People and Customs*, 193.
144 Earle, 317.
145 Warwick, Pitz, and Wyckoff, 239.
146 Swan, 67.
147 Earle, 300.
148 Worrell, 41.
149 Worrell, 45.
150 Linda Baumgarten and John Watson, *Costume Close-Up Clothing Construction and Pattern: 1750–1790* (Williamsburg: Colonial Williamsburg Foundation, 1999), 43.
151 Staples and Shaw, 398–401.
152 David Loranger and Eulanda A. Sanders, "Sumptuary Synergy: British Imperialism Through the Tartan and Slave Trades," *Textile Society of America Symposium Proceedings*, October 2016, 685, Digital Commons@ University of Nebraska-Lincon.
153 James Habersham, *The Letters of Hon. Habersham, 1756–1775* (Savannah: Savannah Morning Newsprint, 1904), 15.
154 Beckert, 101.
155 Staples and Shaw, 154–56.

156 George Washington, *Spinning Report*, August 10, 1793; George Washington, *Spinning Report*, February 16, 1793.

157 Crew, Bunch, and Price, 49.

158 Eulanda A. Sanders, "The Politics of Textiles Used in African American Slave Clothing," *Textile Society of America Symposium Proceedings*, October 2012, 6, Digital Commons@ University of Nebraska-Lincon.

159 Adele Hast, "The Legal Status of the Negro in Virginia 1705–1765," *The Journal of Negro History* 54, no. 3 (1969): 223–24, https://doi.org/10.2307/2716667.

160 Hazard and Shelley, "The Journal of Ebenezer Hazard in Virginia, 1777," 410.

Index

Note: Numbers in *italics* indicate a figure.

R

S

For Product Safety Concerns and Information please contact our EU representative GPSR@taylorandfrancis.com Taylor & Francis Verlag GmbH, Kaufingerstraße 24, 80331 München, Germany

Batch number: 10722112

Printed by Printforce, the Netherlands